Platonic

ALFRED EDWARD HOUSMAN was born in 1859. His most famous work, A SHROPSHIRE LAD, was written in 1896. In later years he became a professor of Latin, edited Manilius' *Astronomica,* and published *Last Poems* (1922). These poems, and those collected posthumously by his brother, Laurence Housman, in *More Poems* (1936) were, for the most part, written during the time he wrote A SHROPSHIRE LAD. He died in 1936.

"There seems to me to be no question as to the enduring quality of A. E. Housman's poetry. I do not think of any living writer whose work is likely to live longer, if as long."
Edwin Arlington Robinson

A Shropshire Lad

A. E. Housman

**Supplementary material by
Dr. Joseph Mersand**

AN AVON LIBRARY BOOK

This Avon Library Edition is the first
publication in any form of *A Shropshire Lad*,
with the additional material by
Dr. Joseph Mersand.

The editors of Avon Books wish to gratefully
acknowledge the assistance of William White
in preparation of *A Shropshire Lad*.

AVON BOOKS
A division of
The Hearst Corporation
959 Eighth Avenue
New York, New York   10019

First Avon Printing, August, 1950
Fifth Avon Printing, September, 1964
First Avon Library Edition (Sixth Printing), April, 1966

Printed in the U. S. A.

CONTENTS

A
Shropshire
Lad

THE LIFE OF
A. E. HOUSMAN

Alfred Edward Housman was born March 26, 1859, at Bournheath, Worcestershire, the oldest of seven children of Edward Housman, a solicitor. The shock of his mother's death when he was only twelve was one of the traumatic experiences which influenced his thinking and his poetry. Another shock was his failure to graduate with honors from St. John's College, Oxford, because he refused to (or did not know how to) answer certain questions on the written examination. Denied an academic career for which he was fitted by his great knowledge of the classics, he returned home, studied assiduously for the Civil Service examinations, passed them, and went to London to work in the Patent Office.

From 1882–1892 he served as a minor official registering trademarks, but he continued his studies in his spare time, and published scholarly papers in the classical journals. In 1892 he was appointed professor of Latin at University College, London, where he stayed until 1911. He then moved on to Cambridge

11

University, and remained until his death in 1936.

His poetry published during his lifetime consisted of two slim volumes, *A Shropshire Lad* in 1896, and *Last Poems* in 1922. Two posthumous collections appeared, both edited by his brother Laurence, *More Poems* and *Additional Poems*. As a scholar, Housman won worldwide renown. His edition of Manilius in five volumes is his most solid contribution to classical scholarship. He also left editions of Juvenal and Lucan, as well as over a hundred scholarly papers. Some of his best prose has been collected by John Carter in *A. E. Housman: Selected Prose*. Since his death in 1936, he has been the subject of several full-length critical and biographical studies and hundreds of articles, the most important of which are listed in the section on Additional Reading.

The Significance
of A. E. Housman

If the significance of a poet can be gauged by the attention which scholars and commentators have given to him, then we may justly say that his significance has been rather impressive. For example, in 1941 Theodore G. Ehrsam compiled in book form *A Bibliography of Alfred Edward Housman*. In 1945 Robert

Wooster Stallman published his "Annotated Bibliography of A. E. Housman: A Critical Study," in which he attempted to bring together for the first time all evaluations of Housman's poetry and poetic theory, 1920–1945. If such a bibliography were to be compiled today the list would be considerably longer. At least two entire volumes have been devoted exclusively to A. E. Housman's achievements: Norman Marlow's *A. E. Housman: Scholar and Poet*, and Oliver Robinson's *Angry Dust*. It is significant that at the centenary of Housman's birth in 1959 an address was given in his honor at University College, London.

A second criterion of the greatness of any poet is the opinion of other poets about him or his work. Thus, Thomas Hardy, himself no mean poet, considered "Is My Team Ploughing" the most dramatic short poem in the language. Furthermore, Babette Deutsch, in *Poetry in Our Time* seems to find tribute to Housman either by resemblances or imitativeness in at least three of our contemporary poets. There are echoes or veiled references to Housman, for example, in Karl Shapiro's "V-Letter" when Shapiro writes about mail day in the Pacific theater of war (the fourth stanza is a particular case in point), and in W. H. Auden's "Time Breaks the Threaded Dances." C. Day Lewis, in an early essay about the poets of his generation, lists as their literary ancestors Gerard Manley Hopkins, Wilfred Owen, and T. S. Eliot. Housman's name occurs very frequently in this list.

Finally, Babette Deutsch, also in *Poetry in Our Time*, sees another example of Housman's influence on a contemporary poet in the works of Norman Nicholson, a writer of the Cumberland region. In Nicholson's *Cleator Moor*, she seems to detect the accents of Housman in the metrical scheme, similar to that used by the older poet, and in the role given to homely diction in such words as "wick" and "segged."

A third gauge of the significance of a poet's work is the frequency with which his work is anthologized. There is hardly an anthology of British literature in the past forty-five years that has not included one or more of his poems. Louis Untermeyer, perhaps the best-known anthologist of poetry in our generation, whose *Modern British Poetry* first appeared in 1920, and whose revisions and enlargements have continued to 1962 with ever-widening success, called Housman's "Loveliest of Trees" (*A Shropshire Lad*, No. 2) probably "the finest lyric in the English language."

We come now to an enumeration of the qualities of Housman as a poet which have made him endure when scores of poets contemporary with him and at that time more popular have been forgotten. It must be remem-

14

bered that the first edition of *A Shropshire Lad* was limited to only five hundred copies— a collector's item now of the greatest rarity. To print a second edition the poet himself had to pay the publisher. Although the critical reviews were laudatory, the sales at first were quite small. It was only with the coming of World War I that Housman's poetry became immensely popular because of its militant masculine spirit.

The qualities that are most frequently mentioned as making Housman's poetry outstanding not only among the poets of his own generation, but among the poets in general are:

1. Purely as poetry, *A Shropshire Lad* is indisputably one of the finest examples of the lyric form.

2. Although some critics have found echoes from the Greek lyricists, Shakespeare, and Heine in Housman's poetry, he actually owes nothing to the poets of his own generation. Lawrence Durrell, whose own reputation has continued to grow, states that Housman's poetry was new in that it was the work of an ironist published in a time when sentimental melancholy was the vogue.

3. Housman's poetry is condensed to the uttermost, stripped of every superfluous ornament, pared and precise.

4. There is a combination of pungent humor and poignancy in everything he wrote.

15

5. His poetry features a seemingly artless but extraordinarily skillful simplicity of tone—perhaps the outstanding virtue of Housman's poetry.

6. Finally, his poetry is almost always song. It is sharpened and it may be acerbic, but it is nevertheless consistent in its song-like quality.

It seems likely that Housman's poems will continue to be widely read although Housman considered his greatest contribution to poetry to be his editions of Juvenal and Lucan, and the minor poet Manilius. There are few who would disagree that at least twelve of his own poems have the authority that is attributed to poetry in the great tradition. Although Housman's poems may be small, fastidious, limited in range and restricted in outlook, they have nevertheless the quality to captivate readers' minds, and many of the poems are about as nearly perfect as lyric poetry can ever hope to be.

THE STRUCTURE AND SPECIAL QUALITIES OF *A Shropshire Lad*

A Shropshire Lad is not a mere assortment of sixty-three poems hastily thrown together to meet a publisher's deadline. Housman arranged the poems in the order in which they appear in the book because to him they represented a unified work. Nesca A. Robb goes so far as to say in *Four in Exile* that it is an ordered sequence: "One might almost go farther and call it a poem, for the more one studies it the more intimately do its component parts appear to be related to one another. They are arranged with extreme deliberateness, so that not only does one theme follow another in logical sequence, but the themes prophesy, recall, and intertwine with each other so that, as one grows familiar with the whole, one comes to feel the closest organic connection between the individual poems."

The Special Qualities

Among the qualities which have made Housman's poems endure when many of his contemporaries have been forgotten are: (1) his wonderful use of the right word; (2) his power to convey his emotion directly and powerfully, (3) his expression of a sense of hopelessness and sadness that afflicts many young people when they face a harsh and bitter world; (4) his exquisite sense of rhythm and music in his lines; (5) his ability to combine "the passionate simplicity of Anglo-Saxon, the splendor and eloquence of Latin"; (6) his universality of appeal, ranging from his love for the beauties of

17

nature to his realization that life is fleeting and that one must enjoy every moment fully, lest death come too quickly and end all.

Sometimes the measure of a writer's greatness can be judged by what he has meant to other great writers of his generation. Some of the few that have spoken are the following:

Edwin Arlington Robinson was one of the first Americans to buy a copy of the first American edition of *A Shropshire Lad* in Boston in 1896. He wrote: "There seems to me to be no question as to the enduring quality of A. E. Housman's poetry. I do not think of any living writer whose work is likely to live longer, if as long."

Richard Le Gallienne, who was himself a contemporary of Housman, said in his review: "The charm of such simple lyric or ballad verse as we find here is hard to convey. . . . It would be difficult to over-praise the exquisite simplicity of these verses."

Hubert Bland, another reviewer of the first edition, said: "In this small volume there are many flawless stanzas and not a few flawless poems."

So much has been said by critics about the influence of the English and Scottish popular ballads on Housman's poetry, that a few of their characteristics may be listed here. Their outstanding characteristic was simplicity. The usual definition of a popular ballad is that it is a "song that tells a story"; and it tells it simply and directly. The language is unfigurative and simple. Conventional epithets are found frequently.

Stanzas consist generally either of a couplet of verses of four accents with alternating refrain; or of four lines rhyming *abab*, of which the first and third have four accents and the second and fourth, three accents. Some of the more popular themes are domestic tragedy, unrequited love, and supernatural occurrence. Examples from *A Shropshire Lad* are selections V, VII, XXI, XXV.

The best ballads are remarkable for their conciseness and conveyance of powerful emotion with a minimum of verbiage. Housman's ballads are among the most popular of the poems in this book.

THE ANNOTATIONS AND COMMENTS

Each of the sixty-three poems in this edition of *A Shropshire Lad* is preceded by some annotation, its nature depending upon the poem itself. In some instances interesting facts about the background or origin of the poem are presented, as in XLIV, which we know was based on a newspaper story. In other instances revelations by Laurence Housman, Katharine Housman Symons, or by the poet himself are offered where they contribute to the undestanding or appreciation of the poem.

Many critics of Housman's poetry have been consulted and their views are included when they illuminate in some way obscure passages or the entire poem. It is interesting to know that there are still many lines in Housman's poetry whose meanings are topics of controversy.

In all instances the editor has attempted to make *A Shropshire Lad* a source of poetic pleasure and stimulus to reflection. For those who would like to learn more about the enigmatic personality who created these poems, a reading list is supplied.

It was customary among the children of the Housman family to climb one of the nearby hills, which they called Mount Pisgah, to watch the beacons (i.e., bonfires) that were kindled on numerous hilltops to celebrate local or national anniversaries. This poem commemorates the Golden Jubilee of Queen Victoria.

There has been some discussion among critics about Housman's meaning in the last line. Was he sarcastic? Frank Harris, who is not always the most reliable interviewer, relates in his contemporary portrait of A. E. Housman that he told the poet, "You have poked fun at the whole thing and made splendid mockery of it." Housman, according to Harris, replied sharply, "I never intended to poke fun, as you call it, at patriotism, and I find nothing in the sentiment to make mockery of. I meant it sincerely. If Englishmen breed as good men as their fathers, then God will save their Queen. I can only reject and resent your—your truculent praise."

I
1887

From Clee to heaven the beacon burns,
　　The shires have seen it plain,
From north and south the sign returns
　　And beacons burn again.

Look left, look right, the hills are bright,
　　The dales are light between,
Because 'tis fifty years to-night
　　That God has saved the Queen.

Now, when the flame they watch not towers
　　About the soil they trod,
Lads, we'll remember friends of ours
　　Who shared the work with God.

To skies that knit their heartstrings right,
　　To fields that bred them brave,
The saviours come not home to-night:
　　Themselves they could not save.

It dawns in Asia, tombstones show
　　And Shropshire names are read;
And the Nile spills his overflow
　　Beside the Severn's dead.

(Continued)

I continued:

We pledge in peace by farm and town
   The Queen they served in war,
And fire the beacons up and down
   The land they perished for.

"God save the Queen" we living sing,
   From height to height 'tis heard;
And with the rest your voices ring,
   Lads of the Fifty-third.

Oh, God will save her, fear you not:
   Be you the men you've been,
Get you the sons your fathers got,
   And God will save the Queen.

Louis Untermeyer, famous anthologist of American and British poetry, calls this "possibly the finest lyric in the English language." William York Tindall describes its merit as "saying what the average man feels but cannot say as he would say it if he could."

To Nesca Robb in *Four in Exile* "Loveliest of Trees" "sets the transience of the individual against the relative permanence of his kind, much as each year's bloom might contrast its own frail beauty with the continued existence and fertility of the tree. There is a freshness of morning and spring in these quiet lines where melancholy and delight interpenetrate like the lights and clouds of an April sky. They depict the moment when youth, emerging from the strange timelessness of childhood, first grows aware of the lapse of hours, and instinctively reaches out to clasp life's joys more closely and to live the hurrying moments with a new and trembling intensity."

II

Loveliest of trees, the cherry now
Is hung with bloom along the bough,
And stands about the woodland ride
Wearing white for Eastertide.

Now, of my threescore years and ten,
Twenty will not come again,
And take from seventy springs a score,
It only leaves me fifty more.

And since to look at things in bloom
Fifty springs are little room,
About the woodlands I will go
To see the cherry hung with snow.

Many commentators have noted Housman's frequent sympathetic references to soldiers. We know that the youngest Housman son was a soldier and actually gave his life for the Queen in the Boer War. To Nesca Robb this poem, as well as "Reveille," repeats the exhortation expressed in "Loveliest of Trees." "In 'The Recruit' the young man is called to seek the military glory that has dignified his fellows; in 'Reveille,' though the military idiom is preserved, the summons comes from life itself, bidding man cast off sloth and taste all the experience he may while the day lasts."

III

The Recruit

Leave your home behind, lad,
   And reach your friends your hand,
And go, and luck go with you
   While Ludlow tower shall stand.

Oh, come you home of Sunday
   When Ludlow streets are still
And Ludlow bells are calling
   To farm and lane and mill,

Or come you home of Monday
   When Ludlow market hums
And Ludlow chimes are playing
   "The conquering hero comes,"

Come you home a hero,
   Or come not home at all,
The lads you leave will mind you
   Till Ludlow tower shall fall.

And you will list the bugle
   That blows in lands of morn,

(Continued)

And makes the foes of England
    Be sorry you were born.

And you till trump of doomsday
    On lands of morn may lie,
And make the hearts of comrades
    Be heavy where you die.

Leave your home behind you,
    Your friends by field and town:
Oh, town and field will mind you
    Till Ludlow tower is down.

This poem has been popular with anthologists. Carl J. Weber, who edited the 50th Anniversary Jubilee Edition of *A Shropshire Lad*, examined twenty-five American anthologies covering the poetry of Housman's period. "Reveille" appeared in eighteen.

An interesting experiment with this poem was performed by Donald A. Stauffer. He asked thirty undergraduates what they saw mentally upon reading the first two stanzas. The various comments are incorporated in Stauffer's *The Nature of Poetry*.

Norman Marlow has studied the literary influences upon Housman more intensively than any other scholar. He says in *A. E. Housman, Scholar and Poet* (p. 21) that he thinks "Reveille" is an allegory. In it, Housman is thinking of the shortness of time in which he must make his name in scholarship. The traveling must be done not in realms of gold but of a drearier metal, the piled books of other scholars.

IV

Reveille

Wake: the silver dusk returning
  Up the beach of darkness brims,
And the ship of sunrise burning
  Strands upon the eastern rims.

Wake: the vaulted shadow shatters,
  Trampled to the floor it spanned,
And the tent of night in tatters
  Straws the sky-pavilioned land.

Up, lad, up, 'tis late for lying:
  Hear the drums of morning play;
Hark, the empty highways crying
  "Who'll beyond the hills away?"

Towns and countries woo together,
  Forelands beacon, belfries call;
Never lad that trod on leather
  Lived to feast his heart with all.

Up, lad: thews that lie and cumber
  Sunlit pallets never thrive;
(Continued)

Morns abed and daylight slumber
   Were not meant for man alive.

Clay lies still, but blood's a rover;
   Breath's a ware that will not keep.
Up, lad: when the journey's over
   There'll be time enough to sleep.

This poem has some of the narrative directness and the humor of the popular ballad. Certainly, Housman tells his story in few words and tells it well. In the study of the literary influences upon our poet, one critic, John Sparrow, thinks the country wooing described here might be that of "the lover and his lass" in *As You Like It* (Act V, iii).

Norman Marlow (p. 84) compares the poem with the popular ballad "The Gardener."

V

Oh see how thick the goldcup flowers
   Are lying in field and lane,
With dandelions to tell the hours
   That never are told again.
Oh may I squire you round the meads
   And pick you posies gay?
—'Twill do no harm to take my arm.
   "You may, young man, you may."

Ah, spring was sent for lass and lad,
   'Tis now the blood runs gold,
And man and maid had best be glad
   Before the world is old.
What flowers to-day may flower to-morrow,
   But never as good as new.
—Suppose I wound my arm right round—
   " 'Tis true, young man, 'tis true."

Some lads there are, 'tis shame to say,
   That only court to thieve,
And once they bear the bloom away
   'Tis little enough they leave.
(Continued)

Then keep your heart for men like me
  And safe from trustless chaps.
My love is true and all for you.
  "Perhaps, young man, perhaps."

Oh, look in my eyes then, can you doubt?
  —Why, 'tis a mile from town.
How green the grass is all about!
  We might as well sit down.
—Ah, life, what is it but a flower?
  Why must true lovers sigh?
Be kind, have pity, my own, my pretty,—
  "Good-bye, young man, good-bye."

Norman Marlow (p. 82) compares the plight of the lover in this poem with the plight of the lover in the popular ballad "Barbara Allen."

Like so many of the poems in *A Shropshire Lad*, this one has mostly monosyllabic, simple words, resembling the language of the popular ballads.

VI

When the lad for longing sighs,
    Mute and dull of cheer and pale,
If at death's own door he lies,
    Maiden, you can heal his ail.

Lovers' ills are all to buy:
    The wan look, the hollow tone,
The hung head, the sunken eye,
    You can have them for your own.

Buy them, buy them: eve and morn
    Lovers' ills are all to sell.
Then you can lie down forlorn;
    But the lover will be well.

The stanzaic and rhythmic forms have attracted critics to this poem. Geoffrey Tillotson called the stanza of this poem "one of the most notable forms" in the entire collection. He was unable to discover any earlier examples of it. However, Ernest Dowson, the tragic author of "Cynara," has used this stanzaic form in his *Verses*, published in 1896, the same year of publication of *A Shropshire Lad*.

Donald A. Stauffer in *The Nature of Poetry* points out that the omission of the word "and" from the last line of the fourth stanza varies the iambic pattern of the line, and this omission "acutely reinforces the shock of death."

Norman Marlow compares the speech of the blackbird with the speech of the Twa Corbies in the famous popular ballad of that name.

VII

When smoke stood up from Ludlow,
   And mist blew off from Teme,
And blithe afield to ploughing
   Against the morning beam
   I strode beside my team,

The blackbird in the coppice
   Looked out to see me stride,
And hearkened as I whistled
   The trampling team beside,
   And fluted and replied:

"Lie down, lie down, young yeoman;
   What use to rise and rise?
Rise man a thousand mornings
   Yet down at last he lies,
   And then the man is wise."

I heard the tune he sang me,
   And spied his yellow bill;
I picked a stone and aimed it
   And threw it with a will:
   Then the bird was still.

(Continued)

Then my soul within me
    Took up the blackbird's strain,
And still beside the horses
    Along the dewy lane
    It sang the song again:

"Lie down, lie down, young yeoman;
    The sun moves always west;
The road one treads to labour
    Will lead one home to rest,
    And that will be the best."

This poem has aroused the interest of many teachers and critics. Cleanth Brooks and Robert Penn Warren in their *Understanding Poetry* quote the poem and ask some stimulating questions. To Norman Marlow (pp. 71–72), this poem is similar in many ways to the Scottish Border ballads. The concentration of a tragic murder in twenty-four lines is truly remarkable. A modern newspaper account would be much longer and less memorable. The last two lines are filled with meaning although they use the simplest words: "And long will stand the empty plate, / And dinner will be cold."

VIII

"Farewell to barn and stack and tree,
  Farewell to Severn shore.
Terence, look your last at me,
  For I come home no more.

"The sun burns on the half-mown hill,
  By now the blood is dried;
And Maurice amongst the hay lies still
  And my knife is in his side.

"My mother thinks us long away;
  'Tis time the field were mown.
She had two sons at rising day,
  To-night she'll be alone.

"And here's a bloody hand to shake,
  And oh, man, here's good-bye;
We'll sweat no more on scythe and rake,
  My bloody hands and I.

"I wish you strength to bring you pride,
  And a love to keep you clean,

(Continued)

And I wish you luck, come Lammastide,
    At racing on the green.

"Long for me the rick will wait,
    And long will wait the fold,
And long will stand the empty plate,
    And dinner will be cold."

Another example of Housman's power to infuse emotion into the simplest language. How much can be read between the lines in this passage: "A better lad, if things went right, / Than most that sleep outside," or "When he will hear the stroke of eight / And not the stroke of nine."

Some excellent examples of the sound-effects of his words are indicated in "gallows used to clank"; "The whistles blow forlorn"; "And trains all night groan on the rail."

Criminals are punished every day, but this is one criminal about whom we should like to know more and in whose guilt we do not believe, thanks to Housman's magical verses.

IX

On moonlit heath and lonesome bank
    The sheep beside me graze;
And yon the gallows used to clank
    Fast by the four cross ways.

A careless shepherd once would keep
    The flocks by moonlight there,*
And high amongst the glimmering sheep
    The dead man stood on air.

They hang us now in Shrewsbury jail:
    The whistles blow forlorn,
And trains all night groan on the rail
    To men that die at morn.

There sleeps in Shrewsbury jail to-night,
    Or wakes, as may betide,
A better lad, if things went right,
    Than most that sleep outside.

And naked to the hangman's noose
    The morning clocks will ring
A neck God made for other use
    Than strangling in a string.

(Continued)

* Hanging in chains was called keeping sheep by moonlight. [A. E. H.]

And sharp the link of life will snap,
 And dead on air will stand
Heels that held up as straight a chap
 As treads upon the land.

So here I'll watch the night and wait
 To see the morning shine,
When he will hear the stroke of eight
 And not the stroke of nine;

And wish my friend as sound a sleep
 As lads' I did not know,
That shepherded the moonlit sheep
 A hundred years ago.

Housman, like all true poets, could look at simple, everyday things and see some new aspect. Thus in stanza 2, we see expressed so well all the many activities with which a day is started in the country. "To start the rusted wheel of things" certainly sums up all that goes on. The fourth line in stanza 4, "Her waving silver-tufted wand," is typical of Housman. Like Homer, he liked compound adjectives, and used them effectively. The final two lines have sometimes been interpreted as autobiographical, although the chances are that Housman was speaking generally.

X

MARCH

The Sun at noon to higher air,
Unharnessing the silver Pair
That late before his chariot swam,
Rides on the gold wool of the Ram.

So braver notes the storm-cock sings
To start the rusted wheel of things,
And brutes in field and brutes in pen
Leap that the world goes round again.

The boys are up the woods with day
To fetch the daffodils away,
And home at noonday from the hills
They bring no dearth of daffodils.

Afield for palms the girls repair,
And sure enough the palms are there,
And each will find by hedge or pond
Her waving silver-tufted wand.

In farm and field through all the shire
The eye beholds the heart's desire;
Ah, let not only mine be vain,
For lovers should be loved again.

This poem resembles in its brevity and language the popular ballads. Norman Marlow (pp. 84–85) sees resemblances to "Clerk Saunders," "Young Benjie," "May Colvin," and "Fair Annie."

Housman, we know, was influenced by the popular ballads and acknowledged that interest. We also know of his high admiration for Heine, who in some of his poems used the same concentrated form, charged with emotional content.

XI

On your midnight pallet lying,
   Listen, and undo the door:
Lads that waste the light in sighing
   In the dark should sigh no more;
Night should ease a lover's sorrow;
Therefore, since I go to-morrow,
   Pity me before.

In the land to which I travel,
   The far dwelling, let me say—
Once, if here the couch is gravel,
   In a kinder bed I lay,
And the breast the darnel smothers
Rested once upon another's
   When it was not clay.

Housman often expressed the permanence of
death, just as he so often expressed the exhortation to enjoy every moment of living. Of
course, many other poets have expressed the
idea of *carpe diem* and its counterpart. What
is distinctive with each poet is his way of expressing these thoughts. What is characteristic
of Housman is his last stanza:

> Lovers lying two and two
> Ask not whom they sleep beside,
> And the bridegroom all night through
> Never turns him to the bride.

The simplicity of the language, the inversions
(i.e., "whom they sleep beside"), and the stanzaic pattern are so distinctly his own.

John Sparrow in his article compares the
view of this poem with that of Ecclesiastes XI: 8.

XII

When I watch the living meet,
   And the moving pageant file
Warm and breathing through the street
   Where I lodge a little while,

If the heats of hate and lust
   In the house of flesh are strong,
Let me mind the house of dust
   Where my sojourn shall be long.

In the nation that is not
   Nothing stands that stood before;
There revenges are forgot,
   And the hater hates no more;

Lovers lying two and two
   Ask not whom they sleep beside,
And the bridegroom all night through
   Never turns him to the bride.

This poem has been popular ever since it appeared. In the twenty-five anthologies consulted by Carl J. Weber, it appears in eleven. Its message is so clear and the words and music so suitable to the message that any comment would seem supererogatory. As an example of the attitude of the Shropshire Lad it is most characteristic.

Students of Housman have searched in vain for any autobiographical parallels in the poems that deal with unrequited love. The discovery of any personal basis would in no way add to the beauty of this one. The lyric is unforgettable just because of itself.

XIII

When I was one-and-twenty
  I heard a wise man say,
"Give crowns and pounds and guineas
  But not your heart away;
Give pearls away and rubies
  But keep your fancy free."
But I was one-and-twenty,
  No use to talk to me.

When I was one-and-twenty
  I heard him say again,
"The heart out of the bosom
  Was never given in vain;
'Tis paid with sighs a plenty
  And sold for endless rue."
And I am two-and-twenty,
  And oh, 'tis true, 'tis true.

This continues the thought of XIII, the consequences of giving one's heart in vain. Housman uses here considerable alliteration. In stanza 2, lines 1, 2, 3:

"Ah, past the plunge of plummet, / In seas I cannot sound, / My heart and soul and senses."

The critic F. S. Lucas, in his *Authors Dead and Living*, mentions these alliterations and their contributions to the poem.

XIV

There pass the careless people
    That call their souls their own:
Here by the road I loiter,
    How idle and alone.

Ah, past the plunge of plummet,
    In seas I cannot sound,
My heart and soul and senses,
    World without end, are drowned.

His folly has not fellow
    Beneath the blue of day
That gives to man or woman
    His heart and soul away.

There flowers no balm to sain him
    From east of earth to west
That's lost for everlasting
    The heart out of his breast.

Here by the labouring highway
    With empty hands I stroll:
Sea-deep, till doomsday morning,
    Lie lost my heart and soul.

In this poem there is the balance between the emotion of the first stanza, and the reinforcement in the second by a concrete example from Greek mythology.

The line in the second stanza "With downward eye and gazes sad" was originally written "With downward eye and bearing sad."

The contemporary poet Stephen Spender has commented on the effectiveness of the second stanza in an article in the magazine *Horizon* for April, 1940.

XV

Look not in my eyes, for fear
   They mirror true the sight I see,
And there you find your face too clear
   And love it and be lost like me.
One the long nights through must lie
   Spent in star-defeated sighs,
But why should you as well as I
   Perish? gaze not in my eyes.

A Grecian lad, as I hear tell,
   One that many loved in vain,
Looked into a forest well
   And never looked away again.
There, when the turf in springtime flowers,
   With downward eye and gazes sad,
Stands amid the glancing showers
   A jonquil, not a Grecian lad.

The late contemporary American poet, Randall Jarrell, was especially attracted to this poem, on which he comments in an article "Texts from Housman" in *The Kenyon Review*, Summer, 1939.

XVI

It nods and curtseys and recovers
   When the wind blows above,
The nettle on the graves of lovers
   That hanged themselves for love.

The nettle nods, the wind blows over,
   The man, he does not move,
The lover of the grave, the lover
   That hanged himself for love.

A rather unusual combination of several strains of Housman's ideas: the sadness in the world, the interest in athletics, the little things in life which may give one pleasure.

The word "thorough" for "through" is found almost universally in ballad literature.

XVII

Twice a week the winter thorough
   Here stood I to keep the goal:
Football then was fighting sorrow
   For the young man's soul.

Now in Maytime to the wicket
   Out I march with bat and pad:
See the son of grief at cricket
   Trying to be glad.

Try I will; no harm in trying:
   Wonder 'tis how little mirth
Keeps the bones of man from lying
   On the bed of earth.

Only two quatrains, but what a wealth of emotion! Without any figures of speech, Housman's emotion comes directly from himself to the reader. In his lecture, *The Name and Nature of Poetry*, Housman said of poetry that its special function was "to transfuse emotion —not to transmit thought but to set up in the reader's sense a vibration corresponding to what was felt by the writer." This poem might well be an illustration of that view.

XVIII

Oh, when I was in love with you,
　　Then I was clean and brave,
And miles around the wonder grew
　　How well did I behave.

And now the fancy passes by,
　　And nothing will remain,
And miles around they'll say that I
　　Am quite myself again.

This poem has been commented on almost since the time it appeared. Thomas Hardy called it "one of my favorites." James Brannin called it "the poem by which the world will longest remember Alfred Housman."

The theme is that it is better for the young athlete to die at the height of his prowess than to wait for the diminution of his powers. Housman has taken this bold and perhaps frightening statement and given it a sustained concrete support through his language. Several masterly examples are found here of the power of concise expression. For example, how much is said in these two lines: "And early though the laurel grows / It withers quicker than the rose."

Cleanth Brooks and Robert Penn Warren in their *Understanding Poetry* print the entire poem and a perceptive analysis. Among other commentators may be included the following: Norman Marlow (p. 44) quotes from Herodotus who has Solon tell Croesus that two young men who died young were the happiest men in the world.

In *The Explicator* (Volume X, Item 6, October 1951) William Bache gives his interpre-

XIX

To an Athlete Dying Young

The time you won your town the race
We chaired you through the market-place;
Man and boy stood cheering by,
And home we brought you shoulder-high.

To-day, the road all runners come,
Shoulder-high we bring you home,
And set you at your threshold down,
Townsman of a stiller town.

Smart lad, to slip betimes away
From fields where glory does not stay
And early though the laurel grows
It withers quicker than the rose.

Eyes the shady night has shut
Cannot see the record cut,
And silence sounds no worse than cheers
After earth has stopped the ears:

Now you will not swell the rout
Of lads that wore their honours out,

(Continued)

tation of "sill of shade," in line 2 of stanza 6 and "the low lintel" in line 3 of the same stanza. C. R. B. Combellack (Volume X, Item 31, March 1952) comments on these same expressions. He says that Housman was thinking of Hades, and that the athlete was a ghost in Hades. To him also these expressions meant the cover of the coffin and the earth above it. Elizabeth Nitchie (Volume X, Item 57, June 1952) refers to carvings of Greek stelae which represent the dead person standing or sitting in a doorway. Walter L. Myers (Volume XI, Item 23, February 1953) comments further on the picture of "And round that early-laurelled head / Will flock to gaze the strengthless dead" in the last stanza. Maude M. Hawkins in her book *A. E. Housman: Man Behind a Mask* (pp. 156–158) gives a detailed analysis of this poem.

We see that not only the poem as a whole but individual lines have fascinated critics. Its popularity with anthologists is obvious. Thirteen out of twenty-five anthologies studied by Carl J. Weber in 1946 printed it.

Runners whom renown outran
And the name died before the man.

So set, before its echoes fade,
The fleet foot on the sill of shade,
And hold to the low lintel up
The still-defended challenge-cup.

And round that early-laurelled head
Will flock to gaze the strengthless dead,
And find unwithered on its curls
The garland briefer than a girl's.

Housman's manuscript for this poem originally read "cressy bank" in line 3 of stanza 3. The change is an example of Housman's acute verbal sense.

This was one of the poems which appeared in *McClure's Magazine* through the interest of Witter Bynner, its poetry editor and an early admirer of Housman's poetry.

XX

Oh fair enough are sky and plain,
    But I know fairer far:
Those are as beautiful again
    That in the water are;

The pools and rivers wash so clean
    The trees and clouds and air,
The like on earth was never seen,
    And oh that I were there.

These are the thoughts I often think
    As I stand gazing down
In act upon the cressy brink
    To strip and dive and drown;

But in the golden-sanded brooks
    And azure meres I spy
A silly lad that longs and looks
    And wishes he were I.

As an example of the care with which A. E. Housman polished his poems we have his "coloured counties" in line 3 of stanza 2. Laurence Housman in *My Brother, A. E. Housman* (pp. 102–103) tells the story:

I asked him once whether, as a rule, his so happily-chosen adjectives had come to him spontaneously or after labour and with difficulty; and I gave as an instance "coloured counties," a phrase which has become famous. "Now, that you should have picked that out," he said, "is interesting. When I wrote the poem I put down, just to fill up for the time, a quite ordinary adjective, which didn't satisfy me; others followed. Then with the poem in my head, I went to bed and dreamed, and in my dream I hit on the word 'painted'; when I woke up I saw that 'painted' wouldn't do, but it gave me 'coloured' as the right word."

This is confirmed in the first draft of the poem which I found in one of his note-books, where the alternatives run: sunny, pleasant, checkered, patterned; "painted" is left out,

XXI

Bredon* Hill

In summertime on Bredon
　　The bells they sound so clear;
Round both the shires they ring them
　　In steeples far and near,
　　A happy noise to hear.

Here of a Sunday morning
　　My love and I would lie,
And see the coloured counties,
　　And hear the larks so high
　　About us in the sky.

The bells would ring to call her
　　In valleys miles away:
"Come all to church, good people;
　　Good people, come and pray."
　　But here my love would stay.

And I would turn and answer
　　Among the springing thyme,
"Oh, peal upon our wedding,
　　　　　　　　　　(Continued)

* Pronounced Breedon. [A. E. H.]

it was not necessary for that to be written down—it had suggested the right word.

Norman Marlow (pp. 80–82) analyzes this poem in considerable detail because to him it represents a poem that could have been written only by a poet who was steeped in the popular ballads. Although there are few direct verbal reminiscences there is a "faint echo throughout."

Housman once explained that "that poem was written early, before I knew the book would be a Shropshire book."

And we will hear the chime,
And come to church in time."

But when the snows at Christmas
On Bredon top were strown,
My love rose up so early
And stole out unbeknown
And went to church alone.

They tolled the one bell only,
Groom there was none to see,
The mourners followed after,
And so to church went she,
And would not wait for me.

The bells they sound on Bredon,
And still the steeples hum.
"Come all to church, good people,"—
Oh, noisy bells, be dumb;
I hear you, I will come.

Another example of Housman's attitude toward the British soldier. It has the simplicity we associate with his poetry.

XXII

The street sounds to the soldiers' tread,
    And out we troop to see:
A single redcoat turns his head,
    He turns and looks at me.

My man, from sky to sky's so far,
    We never crossed before;
Such leagues apart the world's ends are,
    We're like to meet no more;

What thoughts at heart have you and I
    We cannot stop to tell;
But dead or living, drunk or dry,
    Soldier, I wish you well.

An inevitable comparison is between this poem and "To an Athlete Dying Young."

To indicate how carefully Housman re-worked his lines, we know that line 15 originally read: "They carry unspoilt into safety the honor of man." The change to "They carry back bright to the coiner the mintage of man" led Laurence Housman to comment: "Surely in that change one sees in a flash inspiration at work."

Gerald Gould has written an amusing parody, which appears in *Housman: 1897–1936* by Grant Richards.

XXIII

The lads in their hundreds to Ludlow come in
    for the fair,
  There's men from the barn and the forge
    and the mill and the fold,
The lads for the girls and the lads for the liquor
    are there,
  And there with the rest are the lads that
    will never be old.

There's chaps from the town and the field and
    the till and the cart,
  And many to count are the stalwart, and
    many the brave,
And many the handsome of face and the
    handsome of heart,
  And few that will carry their looks or their
    truth to the grave.

I wish one could know them, I wish there
    were tokens to tell
  The fortunate fellows that now you can
    never discern;

(Continued)

And then one could talk with them friendly
    and wish them farewell
    And watch them depart on the way that they
    will not return.

But now you may stare as you like and there's
    nothing to scan;
    And brushing your elbow unguessed-at and
    not to be told
They carry back bright to the coiner the
    mintage of man,
    The lads that will die in their glory and
    never be old.

Another expression of Housman's plea to make the most of life while one is young. More prosaically we say, "We'll be dead a long time."

XXIV

Say, lad, have you things to do?
    Quick then, while your day's at prime.
Quick, and if 'tis work for two,
    Here am I, man: now's your time.

Send me now, and I shall go;
    Call me, I shall hear you call;
Use me ere they lay me low
    Where a man's no use at all;

Ere the wholesome flesh decay,
    And the willing nerve be numb,
And the lips lack breath to say,
    "No, my lad, I cannot come."

Another example of the compact narrative of the ballads. A. F. Allison says: "The curious repetitive chant of this ballad, which gives to an already grim thought an added grimness, is reproduced in lines such as the following: 'Fred keeps the house all kinds of weather, / And clay's the house he keeps.' "

Norman Marlow (p. 79) also refers to the latter line as reminiscent of the language of the ballads, especially "Proud Lady Margaret."

XXV

This time of year a twelvemonth past,
  When Fred and I would meet,
We needs must jangle, till at last
  We fought and I was beat.

So then the summer fields about,
  Till rainy days began,
Rose Harland on her Sundays out
  Walked with the better man.

The better man she walks with still,
  Though now 'tis not with Fred:
A lad that lives and has his will
  Is worth a dozen dead.

Fred keeps the house all kinds of weather,
  And clay's the house he keeps;
When Rose and I walk out together
  Stock-still lies Fred and sleeps.

Professor Tom Burns Haber in studying the verse patterns used by Housman showed that out of 178 published poems all but 47 are in the quatrain pattern common to ballad poetry. This poem is not in quatrains but in two 10-line stanzas, with rhyming couplets in iambic tetrameter rhythm.

The theme—the evanescence of love—is a familiar one in Housman.

XXVI

Along the field as we came by
A year ago, my love and I,
The aspen over stile and stone
Was talking to itself alone.
"Oh who are these that kiss and pass?
A country lover and his lass;
Two lovers looking to be wed;
And time shall put them both to bed,
But she shall lie with earth above,
And he beside another love."

And sure enough beneath the tree
There walks another love with me,
And overhead the aspen heaves
Its rainy-sounding silver leaves;
And I spell nothing in their stir,
But now perhaps they speak to her,
And plain for her to understand
They talk about a time at hand
When I shall sleep with clover clad,
And she beside another lad.

According to Mrs. Florence Emily Hardy, this was Thomas Hardy's favorite of Housman's poems. The reasons are not hard to find. Hardy, too, wrote of lads whose love did not last, but whose fields were plowed and whose work was carried on long after they passed away.

Norman Marlow (p. 54) remarks that "the colloquy between the living and the dead, so magnificently employed in 'Is my team ploughing?' is a frequent device of the Greek epigrammatists, though the influence of the Border ballads is also strong in this respect."

To one critic, Maude M. Hawkins (p. 158), this poem illustrates Housman's belief that true love between man and woman is possible only in a state of matrimony—a lifelong devotion to one mate.

Vaughan Williams set this poem to music but he omitted the football verses, to which Housman objected strongly. "How would he like me to cut two bars of his music?" he asked.

XXVII

"Is my team ploughing,
    That I was used to drive
And hear the harness jingle
    When I was man alive?"

Ay, the horses trample,
    The harness jingles now;
No change though you lie under
    The land you used to plough.

"Is football playing
    Along the river shore,
With lads to chase the leather,
    Now I stand up no more?"

Ay, the ball is flying,
    The lads play heart and soul;
The goal stands up, the keeper
    Stands up to keep the goal.

"Is my girl happy,
    That I thought hard to leave,
And has she tired of weeping
    As she lies down at eve?"

                        (Continued)

Ay, she lies down lightly,
  She lies not down to weep:
Your girl is well contented.
  Be still, my lad, and sleep.

"Is my friend hearty,
  Now I am thin and pine,
And has he found to sleep in
  A better bed than mine?"

Yes, lad, I lie easy,
  I lie as lads would choose;
I cheer a dead man's sweetheart,
  Never ask me whose.

Louise Imogen Guiney, American poet, who
was enthusiastic about *A Shropshire Lad* when
it appeared in 1896, said of lines 13 and 14 that
they have a "grandeur and muffled music which
Milton might have owned."

Commenting on this poem, A. F. Allison says:
"The cruel wars between Saxon and Celt, when
his father 'got him on the slave,' are perpetuated
in the cruel discord of his heart. . . . The open-
ing stanzas . . . are magnificent."

XXVIII

The Welch Marches

High the vanes of Shrewsbury gleam
Islanded in Severn stream;
The bridges from the steepled crest
Cross the water east and west.

The flag of morn in conqueror's state
Enters at the English gate:
The vanquished eve, as night prevails,
Bleeds upon the road to Wales.

Ages since the vanquished bled
Round my mother's marriage-bed;
There the ravens feasted far
About the open house of war:

When Severn down to Buildwas ran
Coloured with the death of man,
Couched upon her brother's grave
The Saxon got me on the slave.

The sound of fight is silent long
That began the ancient wrong;
Long the voice of tears is still
That wept of old the endless ill.

(Continued)

In my heart it has not died,
The war that sleeps on Severn side;
They cease not fighting, east and west,
On the marches of my breast.

Here the truceless armies yet
Trample, rolled in blood and sweat;
They kill and kill and never die;
And I think that each is I.

None will part us, none undo
The knot that makes one flesh of two,
Sick with hatred, sick with pain,
Strangling—When shall we be slain?

When shall I be dead and rid
Of the wrong my father did?
How long, how long, till spade and hearse
Put to sleep my mother's curse?

Another of Housman's *carpe diem* poems,
but made concrete by specific references. At
times this poem recalls the Cavalier poets, Love-
lace and Suckling.

XXIX

The Lent Lily

'Tis spring; come out to ramble
   The hilly brakes around,
For under thorn and bramble
   About the hollow ground
   The primroses are found.

And there's the windflower chilly
   With all the winds at play,
And there's the Lenten lily
   That has not long to stay
   And dies on Easter day.

And since till girls go maying
   You find the primrose still,
And find the windflower playing
   With every wind at will,
   But not the daffodil,

Bring baskets now, and sally
   Upon the spring's array,
And bear from hill and valley
   The daffodil away
   That dies on Easter day.

In this poem Housman portrays the passion of the adulterer. A wealth of suffering is concentrated in such lines as "Fear contended with desire," and "And fire and ice within me fight / Beneath the suffocating night."

Norman Marlow (p. 37) sees unconscious reminiscences in this poem from Matthew Arnold's "Destiny" and his "Lines Written by a Death-bed."

XXX

Others, I am not the first,
Have willed more mischief than they durst:
If in the breathless night I too
Shiver now, 'tis nothing new.

More than I, if truth were told,
Have stood and sweated hot and cold,
And through their reins in ice and fire
Fear contended with desire.

Agued once like me were they,
But I like them shall win my way
Lastly to the bed of mould
Where there's neither heat nor cold.

But from my grave across my brow
Plays no wind of healing now,
And fire and ice within me fight
Beneath the suffocating night.

When Housman used place-names he used them to achieve certain effects. This poem also has many interesting comparisons: the forces of nature vs. the powers of man; the feelings of the ancient Romans and those of the yeoman of Housman's day; the dead past (Uricon) with the living present. How much the poet has compressed in the two final lines: "To-day the Roman and his trouble / Are ashes under Uricon."

Spiro Peterson in *The Explicator* (Volume XV, Item 46, April 1957) explains how Housman's structure transmits and reinforces his theme. That the tensions of Housman's own life are expressed in "On Wenlock Edge" is strongly felt by Maude M. Hawkins. She states (pp. 153–154): "In powerful monosyllables Housman creates an image of the eternal struggle of man and nature with the gale of destiny as symbolized by the Romans and the trees in battle and tempest. He becomes one of the Romans on Wenlock, their brother by heredity and struggle. The trees bent double in the gale are images of his own twisted personality, torn by the irregular nature of his stormy desires."

XXXI

On Wenlock Edge the wood's in trouble;
    His forest fleece the Wrekin heaves;
The gale, it plies the saplings double,
    And thick on Severn snow the leaves.

'Twould blow like this through holt and
      hanger
    When Uricon the city stood:
'Tis the old wind in the old anger,
    But then it threshed another wood.

Then, 'twas before my time, the Roman
    At yonder heaving hill would stare:
The blood that warms an English yeoman,
    The thoughts that hurt him, they were
      there.

There, like the wind through woods in riot,
    Through him the gale of life blew high;
The tree of man was never quiet:
    Then 'twas the Roman, now 'tis I.

(Continued)

The gale, it plies the saplings double,
  It blows so hard, 'twill soon be gone:
To-day the Roman and his trouble
  Are ashes under Uricon.

Another variation of Housman's theme of
the brevity of human life, and the many influences that go into the makeup of a person. He
explains "twelve-winded sky" with his "twelve
quarters" in the next to the last line.

XXXII

From far, from eve and morning
   And yon twelve-winded sky,
The stuff of life to knit me
   Blew hither: here am I.

Now—for a breath I tarry
   Nor yet disperse apart—
Take my hand quick and tell me,
   What have you in your heart.

Speak now, and I will answer;
   How shall I help you, say;
Ere to the wind's twelve quarters
   I take my endless way.

Many critics have praised Housman for his simplicity of language, as well as the magic which that very simplicity casts upon us.

Norman Marlow (p. 136) cites as an example the last stanza:

> But now, since all is idle,
>   To this lost heart be kind,
> Ere to a town you journey
>   Where friends are ill to find.

Whereas most of us would expect "hard to find" as the last three words, Housman chose "ill to find." Some see in this an influence of the popular ballads. Professor G. B. A. Fletcher pointed it out, however, as an example of Housman's avoidance of dissonance.

XXXIII

If truth in hearts that perish
  Could move the powers on high,
I think the love I bear you
  Should make you not to die.

Sure, sure, if stedfast meaning,
  If single thought could save,
The world might end to-morrow,
  You should not see the grave.

This long and sure-set liking,
  This boundless will to please,
—Oh, you should live for ever
  If there were help in these.

But now, since all is idle,
  To this lost heart be kind,
Ere to a town you journey
  Where friends are ill to find.

Another of Housman's poems about soldiers. Housman's interest in soldiering went as far back as 1874–1875 when he wrote to his stepmother from London, where he was spending the Christmas holidays: "The Quadrant, Regent Street, and Pall Mall are the finest streets; but I think of all I have seen what has impressed me most is—the Guards. This may be barbarian, but it is true."

It is considered by some critics that Kipling's *Barrack-Room Ballads* and the street ballads urging enlistment may have influenced "The New Mistress."

XXXIV

THE NEW MISTRESS

"Oh, sick I am to see you, will you never let me
    be?
You may be good for something but you are not
    good for me.
Oh, go where you are wanted, for you are not
    wanted here.
And that was all the farewell when I parted
    from my dear.

"I will go where I am wanted, to a lady born
    and bred
Who will dress me free for nothing in a
    uniform of red;
She will not be sick to see me if I only keep it
    clean:
I will go where I am wanted for a soldier of
    the Queen.

"I will go where I am wanted, for the sergeant
    does not mind;
He may be sick to see me but he treats me very
    kind:

                                    (Continued)

97

He gives me beer and breakfast and a ribbon
    for my cap,
And I never knew a sweetheart spend her
    money on a chap.

"I will go where I am wanted, where there's
    room for one or two,
And the men are none too many for the work
    there is to do;
Where the standing line wears thinner and
    the dropping dead lie thick;
And the enemies of England they shall see
    me and be sick."

The onomatopoeia is particularly effective in this poem. One can hear the sound of marching columns of soldiers in the first stanza. Alliteration is noted in "*B*leach the *b*ones of comrades slain; / *L*ovely *l*ads and dead and rotten."

John Sparrow points to Falstaff's lines in *Henry IV*, Pt. I, IV, ii: "Food for powder, food for powder." That Housman, with his tenacious memory, should recall such lines is not surprising.

XXXV

On the idle hill of summer,
   Sleepy with the flow of streams,
Far I hear the steady drummer
   Drumming like a noise in dreams.

Far and near and low and louder
   On the roads of earth go by,
Dear to friends and food for powder,
   Soldiers marching, all to die.

East and west on fields forgotten
   Bleach the bones of comrades slain,
Lovely lads and dead and rotten;
   None that go return again.

Far the calling bugles hollo,
   High the screaming fife replies,
Gay the files of scarlet follow:
   Woman bore me, I will rise.

Housman here combines sadness of mood with stillness and loneliness. How effectively he creates stillness with "Still hangs the hedge without a gust, / Still, still the shadows stay."

The poem recalls Alfred Noyes's *The Highwayman* with its line "the road was a ribbon of moonlight."

It may seem a very easy thing to write such a line as "The moon stands blank above." However, these perfectly chosen monosyllables enhance the visual effect.

XXXVI

White in the moon the long road lies,
　　The moon stands blank above;
White in the moon the long road lies
　　That leads me from my love.

Still hangs the hedge without a gust,
　　Still, still the shadows stay:
My feet upon the moonlit dust
　　Pursue the ceaseless way.

The world is round, so travellers tell,
　　And straight though reach the track,
Trudge on, trudge on, 'twill all be well,
　　The way will guide one back.

But ere the circle homeward hies
　　Far, far must it remove:
White in the moon the long road lies
　　That leads me from my love.

This is the first of the poems in the collection that is not in stanzaic form. It is iambic tetrameter in rhymed couplets, an unusual rhyme and metrical scheme for Housman.

A. E. Housman wanted *A Shropshire Lad* to be read as a complete sequence, with each poem following in its proper order. With XXXVII his Shropshire Lad leaves his native Shropshire and takes the train to London. As he rides, he looks back to the friends whom he has left behind. He also looks ahead with the firm resolution not to make his friends ashamed of him in his new life in London.

It should be emphasized that Housman was *not* born in Shropshire but in Worcestershire, and that the Shropshire hills were on his western horizon. The natural magic of the Shropshire hills is enhanced by such haunting names as these in "And if my foot returns no more / To Teme nor Corve nor Severn shore."

XXXVII

As through the wild green hills of Wyre
The train ran, changing sky and shire,
And far behind, a fading crest,
Low in the forsaken west
Sank the high-reared head of Clee,
My hand lay empty on my knee.
Aching on my knee it lay:
That morning half a shire away
So many an honest fellow's fist
Had well-nigh wrung it from the wrist.
Hand, said I, since now we part
From fields and men we know by heart,
From strangers' faces, strangers' lands,—
Hand, you have held true fellows' hands.
Be clean then; rot before you do
A thing they'd not believe of you.
You and I must keep from shame
In London streets the Shropshire name;
On banks of Thames they must not say
Severn breeds worse men than they;
And friends abroad must bear in mind
Friends at home they leave behind.
Oh, I shall be stiff and cold
When I forget you, hearts of gold;

(Continued)

The land where I shall mind you not
Is the land where all's forgot.
And if my foot returns no more
To Teme nor Corve nor Severn shore,
Luck, my lads, be with you still
By falling stream and standing hill,
By chiming tower and whispering tree,
Men that made a man of me.
About your work in town and farm
Still you'll keep my head from harm,
Still you'll help me, hands that gave
A grasp to friend me to the grave.

Now that the Shropshire Lad has left his native county and come to London, he can no longer speak with or hear his friends he left behind. Norman Marlow (pp. 55–56) comments upon Housman's last lines: "The quiet words echo in our minds long after we have read them. In this power of conveying meaning and in this capacity to make the last line of a poem linger and move us profoundly, Housman may not have consciously adopted the technique of the masters of the Greek epigram, but the effects they achieve at least move us in a similar way."

Housman changed line ten to read "loose" rather than "thick" in 1922.

What a wealth of emotion Housman has put into his last line "And sigh upon the road."

XXXVIII

The winds out of the west land blow,
   My friends have breathed them there;
Warm with the blood of lads I know
   Comes east the sighing air.

It fanned their temples, filled their lungs,
   Scattered their forelocks free;
My friends made words of it with tongues
   That talk no more to me.

Their voices, dying as they fly,
   Loose on the wind are sown;
The names of men blow soundless by,
   My fellows' and my own.

Oh lads, at home I heard you plain,
   But here your speech is still,
And down the sighing wind in vain
   You hollo from the hill.

The wind and I, we both were there,
   But neither long abode;
Now through the friendless world we fare
   And sigh upon the road.

Another poem of longing for the natural beauties of Shropshire by one who has left them. In the last line of this poem, as well as in others, Housman uses the negative to sum up the bitterness and inevitability of separation and death. Similar negatives are used in XXIV, XXVI, XXVII, and XL.

This poem, we know, was composed in February 1893.

XXXIX

'Tis time, I think, by Wenlock town
    The golden broom should blow;
The hawthorn sprinkled up and down
    Should charge the land with snow.

Spring will not wait the loiterer's time
    Who keeps so long away;
So others wear the broom and climb
    The hedgerows heaped with may.

Oh tarnish late on Wenlock Edge,
    Gold that I never see;
Lie long, high snowdrifts in the hedge
    That will not shower on me.

In the opinion of Donald A. Stauffer in his *The Nature of Poetry*, "no word can be changed without changing the effect of the whole." The characteristics of poetry possessed by these eight lines are: (1) exactness, (2) intensity, (3) concreteness, (4) complexity, (5) rhythm, (6) form.

John Sparrow in his essay compares stanza 2 with Gray's *Ode on a Distant Prospect of Eton College:*

Ah happy hills, ah pleasing shade,
Ah fields belov'd in vain
Where once my careless childhood stray'd,
A stranger yet to pain!

Carl J. Weber in his edition of *A Shropshire Lad* says: "This poem, more than any other, sums up Housman's pangs of remembrance in London, of his home in Bromsgrove and his boyhood there."

XL

Into my heart an air that kills
   From yon far country blows:
What are those blue remembered hills,
   What spires, what farms are those?

That is the land of lost content,
   I see it shining plain,
The happy highways where I went
   And cannot come again.

Housman left his native Worcestershire (as the Shropshire Lad left his native Shropshire) to go to London. There the poet for ten years served in the Patent Office registering trademarks. Although he had a few close friends, he was probably expressing his own loneliness during those dull years as a minor clerk. The contrast between the comfort that nature can bestow and the indifference of mankind in a huge metropolis is memorable.

Housman's sister has indicated that in some of her brother's poems "he throws off the figment of a Shropshire lad and refers unmistakably to his own home and boyhood" in Worcestershire. This was obviously one of them.

Housman does not often write descriptive poetry, but his choices of epithets here are exquisite.

XLI

In my own shire, if I was sad,
Homely comforters I had:
The earth, because my heart was sore,
Sorrowed for the son she bore;
And standing hills, long to remain,
Shared their short-lived comrade's pain.
And bound for the same bourn as I,
On every road I wandered by,
Trod beside me, close and dear,
The beautiful and death-struck year:
Whether in the woodland brown
I heard the beechnut rustle down,
And saw the purple crocus pale
Flower about the autumn dale;
Or littering far the fields of May
Lady-smocks a-bleaching lay,
And like a skylit water stood
The bluebells in the azured wood.

Yonder, lightening other loads,
The seasons range the country roads,
But here in London streets I ken
No such helpmates, only men;

(Continued)

And these are not in plight to bear,
If they would, another's care.
They have enough as 'tis: I see
In many an eye that measures me
The mortal sickness of a mind
Too unhappy to be kind.
Undone with misery, all they can
Is to hate their fellow man;
And till they drop they needs must still
Look at you and wish you ill.

This is one of the earliest of the poems, and was composed in September 1890.

In it Housman represents Hermes in two capacities: as escorter of the dead to their place in the underworld; and as the beguiler of the living, luring them on over hill and dale, but never permitting them to gain their hearts' desire.

To some critics this poem is symbolic and allegorical. The final quatrain bears the unmistakable Housman stamp:

With lips that brim with laughter
But never once respond,
And feet that fly on feathers,
And serpent-circled wand.

XLII
The Merry Guide

Once in the wind of morning
 I ranged the thymy wold;
The world-wide air was azure
 And all the brooks ran gold.

There through the dews beside me
 Behold a youth that trod,
With feathered cap on forehead,
 And poised a golden rod.

With mien to match the morning
 And gay delightful guise
And friendly brows and laughter
 He looked me in the eyes.

Oh whence, I asked, and whither?
 He smiled and would not say,
And looked at me and beckoned
 And laughed and led the way.

And with kind looks and laughter
 And nought to say beside
We two went on together,
 I and my happy guide.

(Continued)

Across the glittering pastures
  And empty upland still
And solitude of shepherds
  High in the folded hill,

By hanging woods and hamlets
  That gaze through orchards down
On many a windmill turning
  And far-discovered town,

With gay regards of promise
  And sure unslackened stride
And smiles and nothing spoken
  Led on my merry guide.

By blowing realms of woodland
  With sunstruck vanes afield
And cloud-led shadows sailing
  About the windy weald,

By valley-guarded granges
  And silver waters wide,
Content at heart I followed
  With my delightful guide.

(Continued)

And like the cloudy shadows
  Across the country blown
We two fare on for ever,
  But not we two alone.

With the great gale we journey
  That breathes from gardens thinned,
Borne in the drift of blossoms
  Whose petals throng the wind;

Buoyed on the heaven-heard whisper
  Of dancing leaflets whirled
From all the woods that autumn
  Bereaves in all the world.

And midst the fluttering legion
  Of all that ever died
I follow, and before us
  Goes the delightful guide,

With lips that brim with laughter
  But never once respond,
And feet that fly on feathers,
  And serpent-circled wand.

For those who are interested in a possible reconstruction of the way in which Housman *may* have written this poem, we advise the discussion by Cleanth Brooks and Robert Penn Warren in their *Understanding Poetry*.

Source hunters have been busily at work here. Shakespeare's "fear no more the heat o' the sun" in *Cymbeline* certainly resembles "Fear the heat o' the sun no more." Recollections have also been noted of Job XIV: 22: "But his flesh upon him shall have pain, and his soul within him shall mourn."

Housman was not often addicted to metaphors, but his effect in the following is unforgettable:

Before this fire of sense decay,
This smoke of thought blow clean away,
And leave with ancient night alone
The stedfast and enduring bone.

In the opinion of Louise Schutz Boas, this poem has been influenced by the poetry of John Donne.

XLIII

The Immortal Part

When I meet the morning beam,
Or lay me down at night to dream,
I hear my bones within me say,
"Another night, another day.

"When shall this slough of sense be cast,
This dust of thoughts be laid at last,
The man of flesh and soul be slain
And the man of bone remain?

"This tongue that talks, these lungs that shout,
These thews that hustle us about,
This brain that fills the skull with schemes,
And its humming hive of dreams,—

"These to-day are proud in power
And lord it in their little hour:
The immortal bones obey control
Of dying flesh and dying soul.

" 'Tis long till eve and morn are gone:
Slow the endless night comes on,
And late to fulness grows the birth
That shall last as long as earth.

(Continued)

119

"Wanderers eastward, wanderers west,
Know you why you cannot rest?
'Tis that every mother's son
Travails with a skeleton.

"Lie down in the bed of dust;
Bear the fruit that bear you must;
Bring the eternal seed to light,
And morn is all the same as night.

"Rest you so from trouble sore,
Fear the heat o' the sun no more,
Nor the snowing winter wild,
Now you labour not with child.

"Empty vessel, garment cast,
We that wore you long shall last.
—Another night, another day."
So my bones within me say.

Therefore they shall do my will
To-day while I am master still,
And flesh and soul, now both are strong,
Shall hale the sullen slaves along,

Before this fire of sense decay,
This smoke of thought blow clean away,
And leave with ancient night alone
The stedfast and enduring bone.

On August 6, 1895, a nineteen-year-old Woolwich cadet committed suicide. He left a letter addressed to the coroner, explaining why he had taken his own life:

I am putting an end to my life after . . . careful deliberation. . . . I will state the main reasons which have determined me. The first is utter cowardice and despair. There is only one thing in this world which would make me thoroughly happy; that one thing I have no earthly hope of obtaining. The second . . . is [that] I have absolutely ruined my own life; but I thank God that as yet . . . I have not morally injured . . . any one else. Now I am quite certain that I could not live another five years without doing so, and for that reason alone, even if the first did not exist, I should do what I am doing. . . . At all events, it is . . . better than a long series of . . . disgraces.

This poem almost quotes the cadet's letter. Laurence Housman found a newspaper clipping about the letter lying in A. E. Housman's copy of *A Shropshire Lad*.

XLIV

Shot? so quick, so clean an ending?
  Oh that was right, lad, that was brave:
Yours was not an ill for mending,
  'Twas best to take it to the grave.

Oh you had forethought, you could reason,
  And saw your road and where it led,
And early wise and brave in season
  Put the pistol to your head.

Oh soon, and better so than later
  After long disgrace and scorn,
You shot dead the household traitor,
  The soul that should not have been born.

Right you guessed the rising morrow
  And scorned to tread the mire you must:
Dust's your wages, son of sorrow,
  But men may come to worse than dust.

Souls undone, undoing others,—
  Long time since the tale began.
You would not live to wrong your brothers:
  Oh lad, you died as fits a man.

(Continued)

Now to your grave shall friend and stranger
   With ruth and some with envy come:
Undishonoured, clear of danger,
   Clean of guilt, pass hence and home.

Turn safe to rest, no dreams, no waking;
   And here, man, here's the wreath I've made:
'Tis not a gift that's worth the taking,
   But wear it and it will not fade.

Housman condemns sickness of soul in the preceding poem and this poem continues the thought. But in this short lyric he is recalling Mark 9:47, and Mark 9:43-45.

Since Housman himself was a parodist, he did not mind when his own poems were parodied. Thus when Hugh Kingsmill parodied both the theme and meter of "If it chance your eye offend you" with such lines as "What, still alive at twenty-two, / A clean, upstanding chap like you . . ." Housman called this parody the best he had ever seen.

124

XLV

If it chance your eye offend you,
  · Pluck it out, lad, and be sound:
'Twill hurt, but here are salves to friend you,
  And many a balsam grows on ground.

And if your hand or foot offend you,
  Cut it off, lad, and be whole;
But play the man, stand up and end you,
  When your sickness is your soul.

Compare this with XXXVII and XLI, which are also in this metrical pattern of iambic tetrameter rhymed couplets.

In XXXVII, Housman uses this pattern to describe his Shropshire Lad leaving his native county for London. In XLI he contrasts the friendliness of the Shropshire countryside with the indifference of the London populace. In XLVI he makes another contrast: between the long-lasting plants which are usually brought to decorate a grave and the short-lived ones which are more suitable to decorate the grave of the young man who has just died. Notice again the negative last line, which has so much force. One critic has seen in Housman's preference for such final lines the influence of one of his favorite Latin poets, Propertius.

XLVI

Bring, in this timeless grave to throw,
No cypress, sombre on the snow;
Snap not from the bitter yew
His leaves that live December through;
Break no rosemary, bright with rime
And sparkling to the cruel clime;
Nor plod the winter land to look
For willows in the icy brook
To cast them leafless round him: bring
No spray that ever buds in spring.

But if the Christmas field has kept
Awns the last gleaner overstept,
Or shrivelled flax, whose flower is blue
A single season, never two;
Or if one haulm whose year is o'er
Shivers on the upland frore,
—Oh, bring from hill and stream and plain
Whatever will not flower again,
To give him comfort: he and those
Shall bide eternal bedfellows
Where low upon the couch he lies
Whence he never shall arise.

Housman wrote two poems about Jesus: this and "Easter Hymn" in *More Poems*. Norman Marlow (p. 106) comments: "In two poems referring to Jesus, Housman seems baffled by His personality but full of pity and tenderness. 'The Carpenter's Son' is deliberately outspoken and colloquial in the mood of *A Shropshire Lad*, but behind the irony there is a passionate, though restrained sympathy, as though Housman too had suffered because of his capacity for affection."

This poem attracted the attention of the contemporary poet Robert Graves, who also commented on the irony in his *On English Poetry*.

XLVII
The Carpenter's Son

"Here the hangman stops his cart:
Now the best of friends must part.
Fare you well, for ill fare I:
Live, lads, and I will die.

"Oh, at home had I but stayed
'Prenticed to my father's trade,
Had I stuck to plane and adze,
I had not been lost, my lads.

"Then I might have built perhaps
Gallows-trees for other chaps,
Never dangled on my own,
Had I but left ill alone.

"Now, you see, they hang me high,
And the people passing by
Stop to shake their fists and curse;
So 'tis come from ill to worse.

(Continued)

"Here hang I, and right and left
Two poor fellows hang for theft:
All the same's the luck we prove,
Though the midmost hangs for love.

"Comrades all, that stand and gaze,
Walk henceforth in other ways;
See my neck and save your own:
Comrades all, leave ill alone.

"Make some day a decent end,
Shrewder fellows than your friend.
Fare you well, for ill fare I:
Live, lads, and I will die."

This poem has interested critics for many reasons. To Louise Imogen Guiney, one of Housman's earliest American admirers, these were "bitter but magnificent stanzas."

Housman's search for *le mot juste* is demonstrated by the word "rive" in line 14. It was arrived at after eight alternatives: vex, plague, tear, wrench, rend, wring, break, and pierce. Laurence Housman said of his brother's poetry, "most of the finest of his poems came with most difficulty."

The handling of the stress in this poem has won the praise of Norman Marlow (p. 63). To him the third stanza has been handled in a masterly fashion.

Finally, the poem's sadness has stimulated much discussion. It is obvious that the poet is speaking from deep anguish.

Maude M. Hawkins (p. 156) finds a biographical element in this poem. "The crescendo element in this poem is very strong," she writes. "The poem has four movements: the first conveys almost indifference; the second, endurance; the third, indignation, as the plight of man and his colossal tragedy impresses itself on the poet; and the last, a mood of complete helplessness against the injustice of the eternals. Here is a Prometheus bound indeed."

XLVIII

Be still, my soul, be still; the arms you bear are
    brittle,
  Earth and high heaven are fixt of old and
    founded strong.
Think rather,—call to thought, if now you
    grieve a little,
  The days when we had rest, O soul, for
    they were long.

Men loved unkindness then, but lightless in
    the quarry
  I slept and saw not; tears fell down, I did
    not mourn;
Sweat ran and blood sprang out and I was
    never sorry:
  Then it was well with me, in days ere I was
    born.

Now, and I muse for why and never find the
    reason,
  I pace the earth, and drink the air, and feel
    the sun.

(Continued)

Be still, be still, my soul; it is but for a season:
  Let us endure an hour and see injustice
    done.

Ay, look: high heaven and earth ail from the
    prime foundation;
  All thoughts to rive the heart are here, and
    all are vain:
Horror and scorn and hate and fear and
    indignation—
  Oh why did I awake? when shall I sleep
    again?

This is a natural companion piece to XLVIII. If man really thinks too seriously about the many heartaches and injustices in this world, he would as soon be dead. Hence it is better not to think too much but have a good time while life lasts. In the last lines of both stanzas Housman achieves a masterly effect.

XLIX

Think no more, lad; laugh, be jolly:
   Why should men make haste to die?
Empty heads and tongues a-talking
Make the rough road easy walking,
And the feather pate of folly
   Bears the falling sky.

Oh, 'tis jesting, dancing, drinking
   Spins the heavy world around.
If young hearts were not so clever,
Oh, they would be young for ever:
Think no more; 'tis only thinking
   Lays lads underground.

This poem incorporates three themes that are frequently found in *A Shropshire Lad:* (1) The nostalgia for the rustic country which he had known as a youth; (2) the troubles one is beset by in a large city—in this case, London; (3) that the only rest will come in the grave.

The names in the introductory verses are those of four villages in southwestern Shropshire. "The stanza is traditional," Housman said.

Norman Marlow, who has studied the literary sources of Housman's poetry, is reminded of Heine's own poignant longing to return to the scene of his childhood (p. 96).

L

Clunton and Clunbury,
Clungunford and Clun,
Are the quietest places
Under the sun.

In valleys of springs of rivers,
  By Ony and Teme and Clun,
The country for easy livers,
  The quietest under the sun,

We still had sorrows to lighten,
  One could not be always glad,
And lads knew trouble at Knighton
  When I was a Knighton lad.

By bridges that Thames runs under,
  In London, the town built ill,
'Tis sure small matter for wonder
  If sorrow is with one still.

And if as a lad grows older
  The troubles he bears are more,

(Continued)

He carries his griefs on a shoulder
   That handselled them long before.

Where shall one halt to deliver
   This luggage I'd lief set down?
Not Thames, not Teme is the river,
   Nor London nor Knighton the town:

'Tis a long way further than Knighton,
   A quieter place than Clun,
Where doomsday may thunder and lighten
   And little 'twill matter to one.

          •

About this poem in particular, Housman's sister Katharine Symons wrote: "Glimpses of the heart-sickness suffered by A. E. H. in London when he went there to live in 1882 are found in his poems. The whole of *A Shropshire Lad* was written while he was there. In some of the poems . . . he . . . refers unmistakably to his own home and boyhood . . . as . . . in No. 51."

We know that while Housman worked in the Patent Office in London from 1882–1892, he often frequented the Reading Room of the British Museum. This poem is, therefore, obviously autobiographical.

LI

Loitering with a vacant eye
Along the Grecian gallery,
And brooding on my heavy ill,
I met a statue standing still.
Still in marble stone stood he,
And stedfastly he looked at me.
"Well met," I thought the look would say,
"We both were fashioned far away;
We neither knew, when we were young,
These Londoners we live among."

Still he stood and eyed me hard,
An earnest and a grave regard:
"What, lad, drooping with your lot?
I too would be where I am not.
I too survey that endless line
Of men whose thoughts are not as mine.
Years, ere you stood up from rest,
On my neck the collar prest;
Years, when you lay down your ill,
I shall stand and bear it still.
Courage, lad, 'tis not for long:
Stand, quit you like stone, be strong."

(Continued)

So I thought his look would say;
And light on me my trouble lay,
And I stept out in flesh and bone
Manful like the man of stone.

This poem was composed in 1891–1892, and refers to Housman's boyhood in Bromsgrove. Fifteen poems from *A Shropshire Lad* appeared in *McClure's Magazine*. This was the first and it appeared in December 1903. Housman creates a vivid picture in his final stanza with his "starlit fences" and "glimmering weirs."

Housman changed line 9 from "long since forgotten" to read "no more remembered" in 1922, one of two textual changes in *A Shropshire Lad* (the other was XXXVIII, line 10).

LII

Far in a western brookland
    That bred me long ago
The poplars stand and tremble
    By pools I used to know.

There, in the windless night-time,
    The wanderer, marvelling why,
Halts on the bridge to hearken
    How soft the poplars sigh.

He hears: no more remembered
    In fields where I was known,
Here I lie down in London
    And turn to rest alone.

There, by the starlit fences,
    The wanderer halts and hears
My soul that lingers sighing
    About the glimmering weirs.

This poem has fascinated many critics and has received extended treatment. Some of them are listed below:

Cleanth Brooks, John T. Purser, and Robert Penn Warren in *An Approach to Literature* analyze the poem in considerable detail and maintain that it is symbolic of the love which has died in the young man; not that it necessarily means that he has committed suicide.

Another theory is expressed by Darrell Abel in *The Explicator* (Volume VIII, Item 23, December 1949). He believes that the poet is saying that the lover in the poem commits suicide rather than prove false in his love.

Maude M. Hawkins, in *The Explicator* (Volume VIII, Item 61, June 1950), feels that this poem is indicative of Housman's attitude toward a woman's love. The woman in this poem is faithless; not the man.

The resemblances to the popular ballad have been noted by John Sparrow, A. F. Allison, Nesca Robb, and Norman Marlow.

Later Maude M. Hawkins gave a different interpretation from the one in *The Explicator*. In her book, *A. E. Housman: Man Behind a Mask* (p. 150) she explains it thus: "Actually this poem is a ghost story! Housman told his brother that the true lover is dead before he begins to speak; he has already cut his throat, and it's only a ghost that whistles, and it's only a ghostly throat that bleeds from a ghost body whose heart no longer beats."

LIII
THE TRUE LOVER

The lad came to the door at night,
　　When lovers crown their vows,
And whistled soft and out of sight
　　In shadow of the boughs.

"I shall not vex you with my face
　　Henceforth, my love, for aye;
So take me in your arms a space
　　Before the east is grey.

"When I from hence away am past
　　I shall not find a bride,
And you shall be the first and last
　　I ever lay beside."

She heard and went and knew not why;
　　Her heart to his she laid;
Light was the air beneath the sky
　　But dark under the shade.

"Oh do you breathe, lad, that your breast
　　Seems not to rise and fall,
And here upon my bosom prest
　　There beats no heart at all?"

(Continued)

143

"Oh loud, my girl, it once would knock,
  You should have felt it then;
But since for you I stopped the clock
  It never goes again."

"Oh lad, what is it, lad, that drips
  Wet from your neck on mine?
What is it falling on my lips,
  My lad, that tastes of brine?"

"Oh like enough 'tis blood, my dear,
  For when the knife has slit
The throat across from ear to ear
  'Twill bleed because of it."

Under the stars the air was light
  But dark below the boughs,
The still air of the speechless night,
  When lovers crown their vows.

Almost a perfect lyric in its classic brevity
and perfect wedding of sound, sense, and
rhythm. Out of twenty-five American anthologies studied by Carl J. Weber in 1946 it was
printed in sixteen. Recollections from Shakespeare's *Cymbeline* have been noted by several critics.

LIV

With rue my heart is laden
   For golden friends I had,
For many a rose-lipt maiden
   And many a lightfoot lad.

By brooks too broad for leaping
   The lightfoot boys are laid;
The rose-lipt girls are sleeping
   In fields where roses fade.

Another of the nostalgic poems in which the poet (or his Shropshire Lad) looks back to the past life "westward on the high-hilled plains." The note of regret for vows that are not kept is found in other poems of Housman.

LV

Westward on the high-hilled plains
　　Where for me the world began,
Still, I think, in newer veins
　　Frets the changeless blood of man.

Now that other lads than I
　　Strip to bathe on Severn shore,
They, no help, for all they try,
　　Tread the mill I trod before.

There, when hueless is the west
　　And the darkness hushes wide,
Where the lad lies down to rest
　　Stands the troubled dream beside.

There, on thoughts that once were mine,
　　Day looks down the eastern steep,
And the youth at morning shine
　　Makes the vow he will not keep.

Echoing in Housman's retentive memory were not only the poems of classical authors, the Scottish border ballads, modern poets like Heine, popular enlistment songs, and the Bible, but such common popular sayings as "He who fights and runs away / Will live to fight another day." John Sparrow shows how Housman took this familiar couplet, changed a word, and pointed a very different moral.

Norman Marlow, in his intensive study of the influences of classical poetry on Housman, found many influences from the Greek elegiac poets (pp. 42–43).

LVI

The Day of Battle

"Far I hear the bugle blow
To call me where I would not go,
And the guns begin the song,
'Soldier, fly or stay for long.'

"Comrade, if to turn and fly
Made a soldier never die,
Fly I would, for who would not?
'Tis sure no pleasure to be shot.

"But since the man that runs away
Lives to die another day,
And cowards' funerals, when they come,
Are not wept so well at home,

"Therefore, though the best is bad,
Stand and do the best, my lad;
Stand and fight and see your slain,
And take the bullet in your brain."

Norman Marlow (p. 100) sees an echo from Heine's "Klarisse."

LVII

You smile upon your friend to-day,
    To-day his ills are over;
You hearken to the lover's say,
    And happy is the lover.

'Tis late to hearken, late to smile,
    But better late than never:
I shall have lived a little while
    Before I die for ever.

The "moonlight pale" is used in several of the poems in *A Shropshire Lad*. What a wealth of emotion and untold story have been compressed into these two quatrains!

LVIII

When I came last to Ludlow
  Amidst the moonlight pale,
Two friends kept step beside me,
  Two honest lads and hale.

Now Dick lies long in the churchyard,
  And Ned lies long in jail,
And I come home to Ludlow
  Amidst the moonlight pale.

Occasionally Housman liked to use archaisms to achieve his effects. "To stir forth free" is such an archaism. Alliteration is here used with the *f* sound, as in such words as "*forth free*" in line 6 and "*far from his folk*" in line 7.

LIX

THE ISLE OF PORTLAND

The star-filled seas are smooth to-night
  From France to England strown;
Black towers above the Portland light
  The felon-quarried stone.

On yonder island, not to rise,
  Never to stir forth free,
Far from his folk a dead lad lies
  That once was friends with me.

Lie you easy, dream you light,
  And sleep you fast for aye;
And luckier may you find the night
  Than ever you found the day.

Norman Marlow (p. 53) sees a close resemblance between this poem and an epigram by Leonidas in the *Greek Anthology:* "Cheerfully press on, going the way to Death; for it is not hard or rough nor full of turnings, but as straight as can be, and all downhill, and is not missed even with eyes shut."

Tom Burns Haber in *The Explicator* (Volume XI, Item 35, March 1953) believes that this poem describes a soldier's death on the battlefield.

LX

Now hollows fires burn out to black,
   And lights are guttering low:
Square your shoulders, lift your pack,
   And leave your friends and go.

Oh never fear, man, nought's to dread,
   Look not left nor right:
In all the endless road you tread
   There's nothing but the night.

That *A Shropshire Lad* was taken literally by many of his readers is shown by the pilgrimages to Hughley to see the steeple. Actually, as Housman had to explain in 1896, Hughley was a village in Shropshire whose steeple was buried away in a valley. The place he really meant had an ugly name, so he had borrowed the name Hughley, because he felt that he "could not invent another name that sounded so nice."

LXI

HUGHLEY STEEPLE

The vane on Hughley steeple
   Veers bright, a far-known sign,
And there lie Hughley people,
   And there lie friends of mine.
Tall in their midst the tower
   Divides the shade and sun,
And the clock strikes the hour
   And tells the time to none.

To south the headstones cluster,
   The sunny mounds lie thick;
The dead are more in muster
   At Hughley than the quick.
North, for a soon-told number,
   Chill graves the sexton delves,
And steeple-shadowed slumber
   The slayers of themselves.

To north, to south, lie parted,
   With Hughley tower above,
The kind, the single-hearted,

(Continued)

The lads I used to love.
And, south or north, 'tis only
    A choice of friends one knows,
And I shall ne'er be lonely
    Asleep with these or those.

Originally Housman had entitled his book *The Poems of Terence Hearsay*. At the suggestion of an Oxford friend, he changed the title to *A Shropshire Lad*. In the first fourteen lines we must imagine a group of listeners to Terence's poetry.

As much as any of the poems in *A Shropshire Lad* this one expresses Housman's philosophy. Yes, says the poet, to get drunk is one way to forget the woes of the world, but when the party is over, there still remains the world with more evil in it than good. Poetry can give one strength to face the world. He concludes with the example of Mithridates who was able to withstand the massive poisons administered by his enemies by taking small doses of poison over a long period of time.

LXII

"Terence, this is stupid stuff:
You eat your victuals fast enough;
There can't be much amiss, 'tis clear,
To see the rate you drink your beer.
But oh, good Lord, the verse you make,
It gives a chap the belly-ache.
The cow, the old cow, she is dead;
It sleeps well, the horned head:
We poor lads, 'tis our turn now
To hear such tunes as killed the cow.
Pretty friendship 'tis to rhyme
Your friends to death before their time
Moping melancholy mad:
Come, pipe a tune to dance to, lad."

Why if 'tis dancing you would be,
There's brisker pipes than poetry.
Say, for what were hop-yards meant,
Or why was Burton built on Trent?
Oh many a peer of England brews
Livelier liquor than the Muse,
And malt does more than Milton can
To justify God's ways to man.
Ale, man, ale's the stuff to drink

(Continued)

For fellows whom it hurts to think:
Look into the pewter pot
To see the world as the world's not.
And faith, 'tis pleasant till 'tis past:
The mischief is that 'twill not last.
Oh I have been to Ludlow fair
And left my necktie God knows where,
And carried half way home, or near,
Pints and quarts of Ludlow beer:
Then the world seemed none so bad,
And I myself a sterling lad;
And down in lovely muck I've lain,
Happy till I woke again.
Then I saw the morning sky:
Heigho, the tale was all a lie;
The world, it was the old world yet,
I was I, my things were wet,
And nothing now remained to do
But begin the game anew.

Therefore, since the world has still
Much good, but much less good than ill,
And while the sun and moon endure
Luck's a chance, but trouble's sure,
I'd face it as a wise man would,
And train for ill and not for good.
'Tis true, the stuff I bring for sale
Is not so brisk a brew as ale:

(Continued)

Out of a stem that scored the hand
I wrung it in a weary land.
But take it: if the smack is sour,
The better for the embittered hour;
It should do good to heart and head
When your soul is in my soul's stead;
And I will friend you, if I may,
In the dark and cloudy day.

There was a king reigned in the East:
There, when kings will sit to feast,
They get their fill before they think
With poisoned meat and poisoned drink.
He gathered all that springs to birth
From the many-venomed earth;
First a little, thence to more,
He sampled all her killing store;
And easy, smiling, seasoned sound,
Sate the king when healths went round.
They put arsenic in his meat
And stared aghast to watch him eat;
They poured strychnine in his cup
And shook to see him drink it up:
They shook, they stared as white's their shirt:
Them it was their poison hurt.
—I tell the tale that I heard told.
Mithridates, he died old.

In his lecture, *The Name and Nature of Poetry*, Housman relates how one afternoon after his lunch while he was taking his usual walk, two verses came immediately. A third came that same afternoon during teatime. However, a fourth verse (not in sequence) did not come until a year later, and then only after thirteen versions. A detailed account of the genesis of this poem is given by William White in "A. E. Housman's Riddle: *A Shropshire Lad LXIII*" (*Mark Twain Quarterly*, Volume IV, Summer-Fall, 1941, pp. 3–4, 21–23).

LXIII

I hoed and trenched and weeded,
　　And took the flowers to fair:
I brought them home unheeded;
　　The hue was not the wear.

So up and down I sow them
　　For lads like me to find,
When I shall lie below them,
　　A dead man out of mind.

Some seed the birds devour,
　　And some the season mars,
But here and there will flower
　　The solitary stars,

And fields will yearly bear them
　　As light-leaved spring comes on,
And luckless lads will wear them
　　When I am dead and gone.

Loveliest of trees, the cherry now
Is hung with bloom along the bough.   II

Now, of my threescore years and ten,
Twenty will not come again,
And take from seventy springs a score,
It 'only leaves me fifty more.   II

And since to look at things in bloom
Fifty springs are little room,
About the woodlands I will go
To see the cherry hung with snow.   II

Clay lies still, but blood's a rover;
   Breath's a ware that will not keep.
Up, lad: when the journey's over
   There'll be time enough to sleep.   IV

If the heats of hate and lust
   In the house of flesh are strong,
Let me mind the house of dust
   Where my sojourn shall be long.   XII

When I was one-and-twenty
   I heard a wise man say,
"Give crowns and pounds and guineas
   But not your heart away;

Give pearls away and rubies
  But keep your fancy free."
But I was one-and-twenty,
  No use to talk to me.   XIII

"The heart out of the bosom
  Was never given in vain;
'Tis paid with sighs a plenty
  And sold for endless rue."
And I am two-and-twenty,
And oh, 'tis true, 'tis true.   XIII

His folly has not fellow
  Beneath the blue of day
That gives to man or woman
  His heart and soul away.   XIV

Oh, when I was in love with you,
  Then I was clean and brave,
And miles around the wonder grew
  How well did I behave.   XVIII

And now the fancy passes by,
  And nothing will remain,
And miles around they'll say that I
  Am quite myself again.   XVIII

To-day, the road all runners come,
Shoulder-high we bring you home,
And set you at your threshold down,
Townsman of a stiller town.   XIX

And silence sounds no worse than cheers
After earth has stopped the ears.   XIX

In summertime on Bredon
  The bells they sound so clear;
Round both the shires they ring them
  In steeples far and near,
   A happy noise to hear.   XXI

Here of a Sunday morning
  My love and I would lie,
And see the coloured counties,
  And hear the larks so high
   About us in the sky.   XXI

They tolled the one bell only,
  Groom there was none to see,
The mourners followed after,
  And so to church went she,
   And would not wait for me.   XXI

That is the land of lost content,
  I see it shining plain,
The happy highways where I went
  And cannot come again.   XL

Oh, 'tis jesting, dancing, drinking
  Spins the heavy world around.
If young hearts were not so clever,
Oh, they would be young for ever:
Think no more; 'tis only thinking
  Lays lads underground.   XLIX

With rue my heart is laden
   For golden friends I had,
For many a rose-lipt maiden
   And many a lightfoot lad.   **LIV**

By brooks too broad for leaping
   The lightfoot boys are laid.   **LIV**

And cowards' funerals, when they come,
Are not wept so well at home,
Therefore, though the best is bad,
Stand and do the best, my lad.   **LVI**

   Why, if 'tis dancing you would be,
There's brisker pipes than poetry.   **LXII**

Oh many a peer of England brews
Livelier liquor than the Muse,
And malt does more than Milton can
To justify God's ways to man.
Ale, man, ale's the stuff to drink
For fellows whom it hurts to think.   **LXII**

Oh, I have been to Ludlow fair
And left my necktie God knows where,
And carried half way home, or near,
Pints and quarts of Ludlow beer.   **LXII**

Questions for Discussion

I

Some critics believe that Housman was being ironic about dying for the sake of the British Empire. Others believe that the poet was expressing his patriotism. What view do you hold?

II

This is one of the most frequently anthologized poems of *A Shropshire Lad*. Why do you think this is so? Is it the idea, the expression of the idea, the music of the lines, or a combination of all these?

III

Most of Housman's poems are written in stanzas like those of this poem. Do you think this an appropriate stanza for this poem? Why? Would blank verse (like Shakespeare's) be more suitable?

IV

Housman has been praised for the vivid pictures in words he drew in this poem. Select the expressions which are most vivid to you and tell what pictures come to your mind.

V

Several of the poems in *A Shropshire Lad* are both narrative and humorous, of which this is an example. In what way does the poet show that he can tell a story and that he sees the humorous aspects of it?

VI

State in your own words what Housman is saying about love in this poem. Do you agree or disagree with him? Give reasons.

VII

Critics have commented on the five-line stanza, which Housman was one of the few of his contemporaries to use. What effects does he achieve with his final lines?

VIII

Housman has told a horror story of murder in a few stanzas. Comment on his power to arouse the emotions and his conciseness of expression. What is the meaning of "And long will stand the empty plate, / And dinner will be cold"?

IX

Housman was moved by hangings and sympathy for the victims. More is left unsaid than said in this poem. What do you read between the lines?

X

There is much action in this poem. How has Housman expressed that activity? Which lines appeal to you most?

XI

Where is the speaker going? How does the poet convey to you that the lover will not remain long on the earth?

XII

In your own words, how would you interpret the lines: "Let me mind the house of dust / Where my sojourn shall be long"?

Both in poems XI and XII the poet is preoccupied with death. How does he reveal this?

XIII

This is one of the most popular of the poems in *A Shropshire Lad*. Why do you think it is so popular? Do you agree with the poet?

XIV

A companion piece to XIII. Do you think it is based on a true experience or is it only a point of view?

XV

If you had not known that Housman was also a world-famous scholar as well as a poet, how would you know it from reading this poem?

XVI

What mood does the poet create in this short poem? How does he do this? By the words, by the rhythm? By the ideas?

XVII

Housman admired the strength of soldiers and athletes. What does he mean by "Football then was fighting sorrow / For the young man's soul"?

Do you agree that it takes little mirth to satisfy a person?

XVIII

One of his briefest lyrics and often quoted. What makes it so universally appealing?

XIX

One of the most frequently taught poems of all of Housman. Why do you think it is so appealing to teachers and students alike? What pictures are most vivid?

XX

What makes this lyric so appealing? Housman used simple, Anglo-Saxon words. How has he been effective in conveying his emotion?

XXI

In your own words, what is the story told in this poem? Housman has been praised highly for his expression "coloured counties" in line 8. What is your opinion?

XXII

How does the rhythm of the poem give the effect of marching soldiers?

XXIII

Housman chose the line "They carry back bright to the coiner the mintage of man" in preference to the original "They carry unspoilt into safety the honour of man." Why is the one he finally chose so much better than the original?

XXIV

How does the thought here resemble II, "Loveliest of trees, the cherry now"?

XXV

What kind of person do you think Fred was? What kind was the narrator?

XXVI

What makes these two lines so vivid: "And overhead the aspen heaves / Its rainy-sounding silver leaves"?

XXVII

What does Housman seem to be saying about love's permanence in XXVI and XXVII? What do you think?

XXVIII

Some critics see in this poem a reflection of Housman's inner struggles. Which lines in the poem seem to bear this out?

XXIX

Compare this poem about flowers with II, "Loveliest of trees," in ideas, style, and beauty of language.

XXX

What do you think Housman meant by "And fire and ice within me fight"? Some critics have contended that Housman was for a time obsessed with guilt feelings which were expressed in some of his poems. Can you detect such feelings here?

XXXI

What are some good examples of alliteration in this poem? How do they contribute to its effectiveness?

XXXII

To whom do you think the poet is talking, and what is he saying?

XXXIII

How would you interpret the last two lines? Who is speaking—a man or woman? May it be either?

XXXIV

Some critics have seen resemblances between this poem and Kipling's *Barrack-Room Ballads*. Read several of the latter and note comparisons and differences.

XXXV

Another one of Housman's poems to soldiers. How does he achieve the effect of marching?

XXXVI

Moonlight and silence set the mood for this poem. How do they contribute to conveying the emotion?

XXXVII

In this poem the Shropshire Lad leaves his native county and goes to London. What parallel do you find between the poem and Housman's own life?

XXXVIII

How has the poet achieved his sound effects in this poem? What does he miss in London?

XXXIX

What vivid pictures of the countryside do you recall from this poem? Compare his description of flowers here with those in II and XXIX.

XL

What is the poet's "land of lost content"?

XLI

What contrast does the poet make between the comfort of nature in his native county and the lack of concern of the people in London? Do you think that strangers in a city—any city —can be lonelier than strangers in the country?

XLII

What is the symbolic interpretation of this poem? Critics have given several. Who is the "merry guide"?

XLIII

Several symbolic interpretations are possible. What do you think Housman is saying?

XLIV

Consult the annotation on this poem. How has Housman taken an event from a newspaper clipping and transformed it into a poem?

XLV

Do you agree with Housman's philosophy here? What authority does he seem to be quoting?

XLVI

Why do you think the poet suggests that only plants that will not flower again should be strewn on this grave? Can you picture the man about whom he is writing?

XLVII

One of the two poems about Jesus which Housman wrote. What attitude toward Jesus does the poet take?

XLVIII

An example of Housman's pessimism. How would you interpret the last line?

XLIX

Do you agree that it is better not to think too deeply if one wishes to enjoy life?

L

What do you think is the "quieter place than Clun, / Where doomsday may thunder and lighten"?

LI

Compare this with Shelley's "Ozymandias."

What does the statue here inspire the poet to do?

LII
How has the poet achieved the effect of nostalgia in this poem? What sound do you hear from "How soft the poplars sigh"? What picture do you get from "About the glimmering weirs"?

LIII
See the annotation for this poem. Several interpretations are given. Which do you prefer?

LIV
One of the most highly praised of all the poems in this book. Can you give the reasons?

LV
What is Housman saying about the younger generation that is following him in his native county? What does he mean by "And the youth at morning shine / Makes the vow he will not keep"?

LVI
What appeals most in this poem: the idea, the expression, or the metrical pattern?

LVII
Another short two-stanza lyric. Compare the

emotional effect here with these other two-stanza lyrics: LIV, XLIX, and XLV.

LVIII

Why should this poem have been set in "moonlight pale"? Compare with the moonlight in XXXVI.

LIX

Compare this with LVIII and XXXVII which also lament lost friends.

LX

What do you think "There's nothing but the night" means? How does the thought here fit in with Housman's philosophy expressed in other poems in this book?

LXI

Can you describe the picture that the poet has drawn? Does it matter that the real Hughley Steeple is not like the one in the poem? Has a poet the right to make such changes to achieve his effects?

LXII

Many quotable lines come from this poem. When Housman left University College, London, in 1911 to go to teach in Trinity College, Cambridge, his students gave him a silver loving cup with the words "And malt does more

than Milton can to justify God's ways to man."
Why was this so appropriate? Why do you
think Housman treasured the cup so much?

LXIII

How is this poem so appropriate as the final
poem of *A Shropshire Lad*? How has Housman's prophecy made in 1896, when the book
appeared, come true?

INDIVIDUAL PROJECTS

1. A Study of the Life of A. E. Housman: See the section, Additional Reading, which follows this.

2. Critical Opinion of Housman's Poetry: Consult the bibliography by Ehrsam which goes up to 1941, and the one by Stallman which ends with 1945. For work since 1945 consult *The Year's Work in English Studies; Annual Bibliography of English Language and Literature;* and the *Annual Bibliographies of the Publications of the Modern Language Association.*

3. The Enigma of A. E. Housman: Start with the biographies by Maude M. Hawkins and George L. Watson and follow through on the references.

4. A. E. Housman as a Scholar: Norman Marlow's study is good to begin with. Then follow through in his references. John Carter's *A. E. Housman: Selected Prose* and A. S. F. Gow's *A. E. Housman* are helpful. In the latter book are listed Housman's Greek and Latin studies.

5. Housman and Oscar Wilde: Housman was working on *A Shropshire Lad* when Oscar Wilde's trial was going on. We know that Housman was stunned by the public outrage against Oscar Wilde and sympathized with him. In the spring of 1895

(when the trial took place), Housman wrote verses which unmistakably referred to the trial. See *Additional Poems* XVIII.

6. Comparison of *A Shropshire Lad* with Housman's *Last Poems* and *More Poems:* What are the similarities? the differences? Did Housman change in his fundamental views of life as he grew older?

7. Housman as a Controversialist: Read Edmund Wilson's essay on Housman in his *The Triple Thinkers* to begin with. In John Carter's book of Housman's prose, you will find several of his prefaces.

8. Housman and His Theory of Poetry: Read his Leslie Stephen Lecture of 1933 *The Name and Nature of Poetry*, published by Macmillan and also included in John Carter's *A. E. Housman: Selected Prose*.

9. The Early Critical Reviews of *A Shropshire Lad:* These are listed in Carl J. Weber's 50th Anniversary Jubilee Edition of *A Shropshire Lad*. For reviews of *Last Poems* (1922) and *More Poems* (1936), see *Book Review Digest* for those years.

10. Musical Versions of *A Shropshire Lad:* See the section on Audio-Visual Materials.

11. Portraits of A. E. Housman: Consult the various biographies. He seems to have admired Francis Dodd's sketch which may be seen in Trinity College.

12. A Study of Housman's Notebooks: Some of these are now in the Library of Congress and may be made available to scholars in that area. An example of Housman's care in revision is found in Cleanth Brooks and Robert Penn Warren's *Understanding Poetry* where his poem XLIII, "The Im-

mortal Part," is analyzed on the basis of the manuscript changes.

13. Housman in Anthologies: It would be interesting to see how many anthologies for high school and college use poems by Housman. Which poems are the most popular?

14. Editions of *A Shropshire Lad:* Carl J. Weber in his 50th Anniversary Jubilee Edition of 1946 lists many of them up to that time. For later editions in America, consult the *Cumulative Book List* for each year.

Additional Reading

BIOGRAPHICAL

Chambers, R. W., *Man's Unconquerable Mind* (London, Jonathan Cape, 1939, pp. 365–386).

Gow, A. S. F., *A. E. Housman: A Sketch* (Cambridge, Cambridge University Press, 1936).

Hawkins, Maude M., *A. E. Housman: Man Behind a Mask* (Chicago, Henry Regnery, 1958).

Housman, Laurence, *My Brother, A. E. Housman: Personal Recollections, Together with Thirty Hitherto Unpublished Poems* (New York, Charles Scribner's Sons, 1938).

Richards, Grant, *Housman: 1897–1936* (London, Oxford University Press, 1941).

Symons, Katharine, et al Editors, *Alfred Edward Housman: Recollections* by R. W. Chambers, A. S. F. Gow, Laurence Housman, Alan Ker, A. W. Pollard, John Sparrow (New York, Holt, 1937).

Watson, George L., *A. E. Housman: A Dividend Life* (London, Rupert Hart-Davis, 1957).

Withers, Percy, *A Buried Life: Personal Recollections of A. E. Housman* (London, Jonathan Cape, 1940).

CRITICAL WORKS

Allison, A. F., "The Poetry of A. E. Housman" (*Review of English Studies,* Volume XIX, 1943, pp. 276–284).

Connolly, Cyril, *The Condemned Playground* (New York, Macmillan, 1946, pp. 47–62).

Lucas, F. L., *Authors Dead and Living* (London, Chatto and Windus, 1926, pp. 173–174).

Marlow, Norman, *A. E. Housman, Scholar and Poet* (Minneapolis, University of Minnesota Press, 1958).

Robb, Nesca A., *Four in Exile* (London, Hutchinson, 1945, pp. 11–54).

Robinson, Oliver, *Angry Dust—The Poetry of A. E. Housman* (Boston, Bruce Humphries, 1950).

Scott-Kilvert, Ivan, *A. E. Housman* (London, Longmans, Green, 1955; Number 69 in the series, *Writers and Their Work*).

Sparrow, John, "Echoes in the Poetry of A. E. Housman" (*Nineteenth Century*, Volume CXV, 1934, pp. 243–256).

Spender, Stephen, "The Essential Housman" (*Horizon*, Volume I, 1940, pp. 295–301).

Walcutt, Charles Child, "Housman and the Empire" (*College English*, Volume V, February, 1944, pp. 255–258).

Weber, Carl J., Editor, *A Shropshire Lad* (Waterville, Colby College Library, 1946; a 50th Anniversary Jubilee Edition).

BIBLIOGRAPHICAL

Ehrsam, Theodore G., *A Bibliography of Alfred Edward Housman* (Boston, F. W. Faxon Company, 1941).

Stallman, Robert W., "An Annotated Bibliography of A. E. Housman: A Critical Study" (*PMLA*, Volume LX, 1945, pp. 463–502).

White, William, 'Alfred Edward Housman (1859–1936)', *The Cambridge Bibliography of English Literature*, Volume V, Supplement (Cambridge, Cambridge University Press, 1957, pp. 604–607).

Audio-Visual Materials

Many of the selections in *A Shropshire Lad* have been set to music, a few of which are listed below. Thanks are expressed to Mr. William Lichtenwanger, Head of the Reference Section, Music Division, Library of Congress; Miss Sheila Crowell of Holt, Rinehart & Winston, Inc.; and Mr. Joseph J. Murphy, Manager of the Retail Division, G. Schirmer, Inc., for help in compiling the following list.

Musical Settings

The Roman numerals represent the numbers of the poems in this edition of *A Shropshire Lad*.

II. *Loveliest of Trees*
   Duke, John (New York, G. Schirmer, Inc., 1934).
   Moeran, Ernest John (Philadelphia, Curwen, Inc., 1932).
   Orr, C. (London, J. & W. Chester, Ltd., 1923).
   Wooley, C. (London, Novello and Company, 1934).

III. *The Recruit*
   Ainsworth, Robert (London, Boosey & Co., 1932).

VI. *When the lad for longing sighs*
   Orr, C. (London, J. & W. Chester, Ltd., 1923).

XIII. *When I was one-and-twenty*
>Debeer, Alan (London, J. & W. Chester, Ltd., 1936).
>
>Freed, Isadore (Southern Music Pub. Co., 1960).
>
>Kalmanoff, Martin (Skidmore Choral Library, 1959).
>
>Robinson, Clarence (New York, G. Schirmer, Inc., 1950).
>
>Wedberg, Conrad F. (Chicago, Clayton F. Summy Company, 1946).
>
>Whitcomb, Mervin; with his setting for *Oh, when I was in love* (New York, Bourne, Inc., 1953).

XVIII. *Oh, when I was in love with you*
>Orr, C. (London, Oxford University Press, 1928).
>
>Whitcomb, Mervin (New York, Bourne, Inc., 1953).

XXI. *Bredon Hill* or *In summertime on Bredon*
>Duke, John (New York, G. Schirmer, Inc., 1934).
>
>Gray, Alan (London, Oxford University Press, 1936).
>
>Twigg, D. (York, Banks & Son, 1936).
>
>Ward-Casey, S. (York, Banks & Son, 1936).

XXIII. *The lads in their hundreds*
>Orr, C. (London, Stainer & Bell, Ltd., 1937).

XXVII. *Is my team ploughing?*
>Orr, Co. (London, Oxford University Press, 1927).

XXXV. *On the idle hill of summer*
  Ainsworth, Robert (London, Boosey & Co., 1939).

XXXVI. *White in the moon the long road lies*
  Fox, Oscar J. (New York, Carl Fischer, 1932).

XXXIX. *'Tis time, I think by Wenlock town*
  Armstrong, Thomas (Philadelphia, Curwen, Inc., 1934).
  Orr, C. (London, J. & W. Chester, Ltd., 1923).

XLVII. *The Carpenter's Son*
  Orr, C. (London, J. & W. Chester, Ltd., 1932).

Bullemorth, George, *Six Songs from "A Shropshire Lad"* (New York, G. Schirmer, Inc.).

Orr, C., *Cycle of Songs from A Shropshire Lad:* "Along the field," "When I watch the living meet," "The Lent Lily," "Farewell to barn," "Oh fair enough," "Hughley Steeple," "When smoke stood up." (London, J. & W. Chester, Ltd., 1934).

Williams, Ralph Vaughan
  On Wenlock Edge; cycle of six songs on poems by Housman (New York, Boosey and Hawkes, 1946).

Recordings

Several of the poems in *A Shropshire Lad* have been recorded in connection with their appearance in anthologies studied in high schools. Harcourt, Brace & World, Inc., has issued the following albums:

Many Voices, contains "With rue my heart is laden" read by Alexander Scourby.

Many Voices, 12A, contains "To an Athlete Dying Young" read by Brian O'Doherty.

Caedmon Records has made recordings for the literature series published by Houghton, Mifflin, including:

The Sound of Literature, HMLS 102, contains "When I was one-and-twenty."

The Sound of Literature, HMLS 104, contains "To an Athlete Dying Young."

Scott, Foresman has issued an album No. 3168 to accompany the anthology *England and Literature*. The selection included is "Is my team ploughing?"